ConFeSSioNS
of a
MaDdog

ConFeSSioNS of a MaDDog

A Romp through the High-flying
Texas Music and Literary Era of
the Fifties to the Seventies

• • •

Jay Dunston Milner

Foreword by Larry L. King

University of North Texas Press
Denton, Texas

Requests for permission to reproduce material from
this work should be sent to:
Permissions
University of North Texas Press
PO Box 311336
Denton, TX 76203-1336
940-565-2142

The paper used in this book meets the minimum requirements
of the American National Standard for Permanence of Paper for
Printed Library materials, Z39.48.1984.

Library of Congress Cataloging-in-Publication Data
Milner, Jay Dunston, 1923–
Confessions of a maddog: a romp through the high-flying Texas
music and literary era of the fifties to the seventies / Jay Dunston
Milner ; foreword by Larry L. King.
p. cm.
ISBN 1-57441-050-4 (cloth : alk. paper)
1. Milner, Jay Dunston, 1923–   . 2. Milner, Jay Dunston, 1923–
—Friends and associates. 3. Popular culture—Texas—History—20th
century. 4. Texas—Intellectual life—20th century. 5. Journalism
teachers—Texas—Biography. 6. Journalists—United States—Biography.
7. Authors, American—Texas—Biography. 8. Musicians—Texas—
Biography.   I. Title.

PN4874.M52A3   1998   98-23419
976.4'063'0922—dc21   CIP

Design by Accent Design and Communications

To Gail, without whose presence, encouragement and advice this would never have been completed.

CoNtenTs

Foreword

When I first met Jay Milner, dinosaurs and the one-and-only original Hank Williams were a long time dead; John F. Kennedy and William Faulkner only recently so. Lyndon Johnson, Martin Luther King, Bobby Kennedy, Jackie Gleason, Red Foley, Chet Huntley and a rowdy bunch of hard-drinking, pot-smoking, lady-chasing Texas writers—many of whom make appearances in this book—were alive and semi-well. So were our dreams—collectively and individually—of soon running Norman Mailer out of town, embarrassing Kurt Vonnegut into retirement and reducing Saul Bellow to full-time school teaching.

It didn't exactly happen that way, but my-oh-my didn't we have a good time *trying*?

I was but a broth of a boy—well, only thirty-five, which seems younger with each passing year—when my path converged with Jay Milner's. The year was 1964 and the place was Washington, D.C. Both Milner and King were repairing their hearts after first marriages that had ended on notes more sour than are heard in "Here Comes the Bride"; Milner was trying to revive his writing career and I was attempting to start one. Our respective Net Worths ranged somewhere between $2 and 45¢, not counting the odd penny.

Jay Milner was my superior in all measureable ways: he had accomplished a first novel, *Incident at Ashton*, published in 1961 by a New York publishing house while I was merely hoping to publish my first novel, *The One-Eyed Man*. He had been a reporter and editor at first-class newspapers including *The New York Herald-Tribune*, while I could boast only of experience on small daily newspapers in desert West Texas and a particularly arid corner of New Mexico. He knew famous folk, including the legendary editor Stanley Walker, the populist muck-raking Mississippi editor Hodding Carter, and New York women who spoke French; I knew only a few pissant garden-variety Texas Congressmen and some West Texas gals with nasal accents and cowboy boots who aspired to be rodeo barrel-riders. It is fair to say that I looked up to Milner and begged his professional secrets both as Writer and as Lothario.

Each of us, it must be confessed, was then living in "reduced circumstances," or—bluntly put—dodging court orders to pony up our alimony and/or child support payments. These obligations were less than easily met. Milner was writing Washington dispatches for *The Fort Worth Star-Telegram* at space rates while scheming a second novel; I was drawing a whole $15 per article for liberal rantings in *The Texas Observer*, when not attending to my own misshapen fiction. I lived in a basement dungeon in a rooming house masquerading as a hotel— The Dodge House—while Jay occupied equally modest quarters in a decrepit hotel three or four blocks away on the opposite side of the grand, glorious and looming U.S. Capitol. Often we shared cheese-and-cracker or baloney sandwich lunches while balefully observing Senators and Congressmen being chauffered to better culinary fare at Duke Zeibert's, The Palm, or other posh restaurants where—we felt certain—*they* would not wash down their food with buttermilk kept on an air-cooled window ledge. Had we known where to go to enlist, I am sure that in such sour moments we might have joined the Communist Party.

Through talent, dedication, perseverance, clean living and perhaps a great deal of blind luck, we both went on to careers that surely astonished our critics and may even have semi-pleased our old mothers. Each of us wrote for magazines and newspapers while nursing our book manuscripts; Milner even *founded* a country music magazine and edited an "underground" newspaper, back when such publications were not only tolerated but fashionable. He was a semi-star on a PBS television station and a truly fine teacher of journalism at TCU and SMU and even worked a stint as a public relations honcho and midnight companion of the legendary Willie Nelson.

Through it all we stayed in touch, laughed more than we cried, and caroused with many Texas writers who appear in this book—Edwin (Bud) Shrake, Billie Lee Brammer, Gary Cartwright and Dan Jenkins among them—as well as professional football players; newsmen and newswomen; artists who painted, artists who picked guitars, and artists who scammed; Fort Worth gangsters; politicians; some few ladies who sold love; and many boys and girls who seemed to have no visible means of support. Hemingway might have called it "a moveable feast," though probably it came closer to being a traveling circus or medicine show. At any rate, it was great fun and I am delighted that Jay Milner has put much of it down on paper in his own irrepressible style. (And, believe me, I am *equally* grateful for certain things he left out; in fact, I been thinkin' of sendin' him money.)

Nonetheless, Jay Milner has crafted an honest book, one that speaks to his time and his place in a clear voice. His recollections of West Texas—my own home territory—in the 1930s and 1940s are vivid and accurate as to topography, mores and the prevailing culture; Jay simply takes me back to my roots and revives precious memories I had thought a long time dead. To the oil fields, high school football, World War II, the dreams and angst of teenagers who mistakenly think they are the first ever to have experienced their splendid miseries, and much much more.

Milner's book is equally true to later periods and to a Texas literary era that we had the good luck to get in on at its outset, a time before our native state had many writers and no small presses, *Texas Observers* or *Texas Monthlys* at all. So this book is valuable in terms of early eye-witness reports and marking change in a time when Texas rapidly shifted from a rural, agrarian society to being among the most urbanized of the fifty states; it spans a period from when Texas was largely a cultural wasteland to a more sophisticated and varied era. It fills gaps and adds vital mortars.

I hope you, the reader, will enjoy *Confessions of a Maddog* as much as I have. And I believe you will.

Larry L. King
Washington, D.C.

Acknowledgments

My lovely wife, Gail, is the one whose love and assistance got me through the actual writing of this recollection, but the following friends were instrumental, in ways they may or may not know, in getting me through the crazy and not-so-crazy times recalled and reflected upon herein: Susan Walker, who kept me posted during my exile and was Best Person at our wedding; Joe Murray, who kept insisting I write again and provided me with my first word processor; Willie Nelson and Paul English, who unknowingly helped lift me out of my lowest years; Cookie and all the merry Maddogs who came and went in my life after I returned to Texas at the outbreak of the pivotal 1960s. And, of course, good old Billie Lee, who died for our sins.

Disclaimer

The people and places in this story are enigmas of my imagination. If there are places named Lubbock, Dallas, Fort Worth, Austin and Lufkin, in a state called Texas, I do not recall ever being there. If there are people in those places with names similar to or the same as characters in my story, it must be coincidence, although I admit being somewhat burdened by short and long term memory loss.

Jay Dunston Milner
Fort Worth, Texas

Maddog, Inc.
Doing Indefinable Services to Mankind

Susan Walker was in charge. In the years after the charter members had passed their physical prime, she usually ran the show whenever a Maddog, Inc. general gathering occurred. It hadn't always been that way. There was a time—in the sixties and most of the seventies—when the founding brothers and sisters of the Maddog fellowship eagerly came together from afar at the most trifling excuse, but that was then, and this was 1987.

The last time the whole gang, including wives and mothers, had gathered may have been back in the mid-sixties when a fellow Maddog was on trial for allegedly giving an undercover narc a joint. Happily, in the indefinable services to mankind tradition, our fellow Maddog refused to accept the money the narc tried to force him to take—or the case might not have been dismissed, in spite of the extraordinary legal services of loyal Maddog, Warren Burnet, attorney of record for the defense. In those days, possession of one joint was a felony, not a misdemeanor.

But I digress . . .

On this particular day, in November of 1987, Susan Walker (nee Streit) was in charge, and the reason everybody and their mothers, wives, children (and even a couple of ex-wives and former mistresses) were assembled there was for the formal ceremony and attendant sideshow marking the historic occasion of the embedding of the illustrious names of Bud Shrake, Dan Jenkins, Larry L. King and Gary Cartwright in the sidewalk along Sixth Street, the Bourbon Street of Austin. They called it the "Walk of Stars," like the one in Hollywood. This was the second group of Texas Stars to have their names inscribed in cement there. The initial group included former University of Texas Longhorn coach Darrell Royal, UT football legends Earl Campbell and Bobby Layne, and singer-songwriter Willie Nelson, a member in good standing of Maddog, Inc., himself.

So, on this fine, sunny Texas hill country day, Jerry Jeff Walker, Susan's singing songwriting husband and an old running buddy of the honorees (a living legend in his own right, whose name would soon be inscribed on that same sidewalk) was master of ceremonies. Being a real pro, he had rehearsed his ad-libs all morning at home and had them down pat. But, as fickle fate would have it, those who were even a few feet away from him couldn't hear a word of Jerry Jeff's clever offhand comments above the rattle, boom, grind and honk of traffic and street repairs going on nearby. This part of the festivities was conducted outdoors in front of a Sixth Street bar.

But he persisted, introducing those who would present those whose names would soon be immortalized in the concrete, for music lovers and revelers to walk upon and stumble over. And as Cartwright said in his acceptance speech, for "countless numbers of students, tourists, winos and pigeons" to do with as they might.

Future Texas governor Ann Richards praised Shrake as a talented and perceptive writer of movies and books and a gentle man. Mike Blackman, an editor at the *Fort Worth Star-Telegram* and fellow West Texan, acclaimed King as a Texas Tech University dropout who had gone on to become one of the country's best known magazine writers and celebrated author of the hit Broadway musical *Best Little Whorehouse in Texas,* as well as other plays and several books. Jenkins was inducted by Darrell Royal and David Burgin, the latter the editor of the late, lamented *Dallas Times-Herald* where Jenkins's weekly syndicated columns were based. Cartwright's induction speeches included the observations of Greg Curtis, editor of *Texas Monthly* magazine, where Cartwright was a senior editor. Blackie Sherrod told a sampling of wild tales about all three. Sherrod pointed out that his former employees, Shrake, Cartwright and Jenkins, had gotten started as sportswriters but had gone on to cover loftier subjects, such as dope smuggling, chicken-fried steak and mass murder.

Although he had been dead almost a decade, Billie Lee Brammer was mentioned several times that afternoon. It was agreed that Brammer and his magnificent novel *The Gay Place* were about as representative of Austin's unique ambiance as could be found.

A number of events were scheduled around the main ceremony outside the Sixth Street bar where circular name plates were secured into chiseled-out depressions in the sidewalk. But the coziest, most enjoyable talk took place in the lobby bar of the old Driskill Hotel. It was there the honorees and their guests casually congregated before and after each event on the formally scheduled program, some drinking Diet Coke in deference to their tired livers or promises to wives and mothers, others sipping the real stuff with more caution than derring-do of former Maddog gatherings.

One twilight, while waiting in the Driskill bar for limos to take them to a reception somewhere, Susan Walker, Jodi Gent, Gary and Phylis Cartwright and Dan and June Jenkins, in their blue blazers and basic black dresses, respectively, languished around a sofa chatting, when a barefooted, scraggly Austin throwback staggered in from the street and fell to the floor at the feet of the group. His thousand-yard stare landed on Susan, and he rose to his knees and whispered something incoherent into her ear before a hotel employee scurried up and hustled him back outside. The well-dressed group watched silently as the brief drama evolved. Then Jenkins said, "Ten years ago, that's the fellow we'd have been waiting for."

● ● ●

Back before there was a formal organization by that name, Blackie Sherrod, whom many called the best sports columnist in America, was boss of the core of Maddog, Inc. founders. By 1987, Blackie more accurately could have been called "Whitey," but was still unofficially deferred to. He was sports editor of the old *Fort Worth Press*, and Jenkins, Shrake and Cartwright made up the majority of his staff. They all followed Sherrod to Dallas in the late 1950s. They were all in Dallas when I came back to Texas from the soon-to-fold *New York Herald Tribune*.

I don't remember the third night I ever spent in Dallas, but I do recall, very clearly, the first and second nights. My first night, I was a member of the no doubt famous "Cinderella Kids" football team from Lubbock High, and we were in Big D to beat the Waco High team in the Cotton Bowl for the state championship. That was in December of 1939. The second night I spent in Dallas was in the fall of 1961, the day I met Shrake, Cartwright and Jenkins. I didn't get much sleep either night.

Shrake and I had the same New York literary agent, a nice lady who, when she found out I was heading back to Texas, told me to be sure and look up this nice young writer who also was a client of hers, Edwin Shrake. I put off contacting him as long as I could, of course, the way you do when an older lady tells you to look up a nice boy she knows. Turns out Shrake put it off as long as he could, too. But finally, he sent me game tickets for the brand new pro football Dallas Cowboys team. It was almost half-time at the Cotton Bowl when I realized the tall fellow sitting next to me with the large thermos was Shrake, and about that time, he realized I was his guest. Shrake introduced me to his first wife, Joyce, and to Cartwright and his first wife, Barbara. He then offered me a drink from the thermos, which I discovered was filled with apple juice and vodka.

When I came upon the scene, the loose-knit group that would one day be known as the Maddog, Inc. founding members already had taken shape in Dallas—maybe even before that, in Fort Worth. Jenkins and Shrake had known each other as students at Paschal High in Fort Worth and later at Texas Christian University there. Cartwright had joined them at the *Fort Worth Press*.

At about that time, Billie Lee Brammer was back in Austin, savoring the afterglow of well-nigh universal acclamation for *The Gay Place*. Pete Gent was playing tight end for the Dallas Cowboys. Larry McMurtry had sold his first novel, *Horseman Pass By*, to the movies, where they changed the title to *Hud*. Willie Morris was editor of *The Texas Observer* in

Austin and writing occasional pieces for *Harper's*. Larry L.
King was still tub thumping for a congressman from West Texas
in Washington, D. C. And A. C. Greene was putting out editorial pages and book pages at the *Dallas Times-Herald*.

So, the momentum was already in place. They were writing, or thinking about writing, and already into a lifestyle that
would carry them to both coasts (Jenkins would give rise to
the "Left and Right Coasts" designation in the not-too-distant
future) and merge with the high-living beautiful people in
Manhattan and Los Angeles. As Willie Nelson, who sang what
he wrote, would do years later, they were building a base of
support at home, and the fact that their fame began to spread
was almost incidental. They fabricated their own myths and
legendary characters themselves from their own ranks.

As a journalist, primarily, I was attracted to this group of
merry pranksters who aspired to literary eminence as a story.
A darn good story, as a matter of fact. Almost as good, on
another level, as the story I had found myself covering in
Mississippi in the 1950s. In those days, I could never walk
away from a good story.

From Mississippi in the aftermath of the 1954 Supreme
Court decision outlawing racially segregated public schools, I
went to New York City where, among other things, I covered
the beginnings of an American folk music uprising. This go-
round, leading folk singers included young Bobby Dylan; Joan
Baez; Peter, Paul and Mary; and other individuals and groups
who were taking folk music in a new direction. Or maybe it
wasn't all that different than the direction taken in the Great
Depression by Woody Guthrie and others who lived what they
wrote about, more or less. For one thing, the new folk music's
instrumental support was better (at least partially because
the record-buying public had more money to buy the records
made by these new folkies). Unlike Depression folk music,

this time the issue wasn't so much physical starvation as spiritual starvation. This time around, too, more of the singing social poets were able to make a living wage than those in the thirties, when nobody but the rich had any extra money. There was room for more minstrels in the sixties than in the 1930s, when just a handful spread the word of the Dust Bowl and the Okies heading west, and what they found in California instead of streets paved with gold.

The 1950s folk music blip was something altogether different. It was more commercial, cocktail lounge stuff, with the Kingston Trio, Harry Belafonte, and others singing the slicked up folk songs from other eras and other countries. This gutsier 1960s version was being composed and sung by young men and women who were disturbed by what they saw going on around them, by the climbing degree of greed becoming evident in the bright aura of prosperity that followed World War II.

My job at the *New York Herald Tribune* was as assistant to the editor of the editorial page, Dwight Sargent. I wrote a Sunday column about folk music and musicians for our entertainment editor, Judith Crist, so I could get into the performances free and get backstage to interview the singers. I've always been fascinated by people who are the best at what they do, whether or not they are immediately recognized as the best.

I barely missed discovering Bobby Dylan for the nation's mainstream just because, well . . . because I procrastinated. People whose judgment and taste I admired kept telling me I should go down in the Village and hear this kid who made up songs from that day's newspaper headlines, and I intended to do so.

But the distracting rumors that the *Tribune* was about to fold were getting hotter, and my associates on the editorial page and in the newsroom always seemed to be talking about where they were hoping to land after the crash and asking me what my plans were. I thought about it and thought about it and came to the conclusion I wanted, under the circumstances, to go home to Texas. The truth is I never really felt at home in Manhattan. I loved working at the *Herald Tribune*. It was a great newspaper, a writer's newspaper, and I appreciated and admired the people I worked with there. But an old lady down the hall from where I lived had died and nobody noticed for almost a week. When they busted into her apartment, they found her body amid head-high stacks of newspapers and magazines. My apartment was beginning to resemble hers, I thought with alarm, and decided to get out of that big, impersonal city and back to the open country of home.

A guy from the *New York Times* was the first to write about Bobby Dylan in the mainstream press. Every time I read about Dylan after that, the guy from the *Times* was quoted, and it teed me off at myself. But, as the great Satchel Paige advised us all: "Don't look back—something might be gaining on you."

So, anyhow, when I returned to Texas in the fall of 1961, before I could get back to my old haunts in the Panhandle and the friends from my childhood days, you might say I fell in with a rowdy crowd of city boys who—of all things—wanted to write for a living. It was as if I had stumbled into something that had been going on for some time. I just came along and latched onto it as it moved by the place where I stood at that moment. Like a train. I hopped it because it appeared to be heading in a direction I thought I wanted to go, had wanted to go for a long time, maybe subconsciously, because for a long time, I seemed to have been scratching this itch that I had somehow missed out on the really fun parts of being a young man. I had been a Good Boy all my life, and the idea of hanging out with outlaws was somehow appealing, even if they were only intellectual outlaws.

We had to know what was going on—in town, and in Texas and in America—among all the people we regarded as interesting and knowledgeable in our sphere of interests, which included music, journalism, contemporary literature, art, sports and such accessory pastimes as dabbling in mind-altering chemicals, casual sex and politics. We kept in touch with like-minded people wherever they might be. We usually urged those in faraway places to move to Texas. We wanted as many attractive, like-minded people as possible as close by as possible—for various reasons, not all of them unselfish.

We kept up with similarly feathered birds of several generations, who were doing their things from coast to coast. We spread the word—sometimes rumors and occasionally actual facts—by word of mouth (some of us were very mobile), underground press, rock lyrics and puredee gossip. We had to hear every new album of significance, and that generally was not the music that made the Top 40 lists. (If this was a portent of who eventually would win the war of minds, we didn't notice it, or chose to ignore it.)

This was the sixties, man. We were older than the kids at the barricades, but there was a feeling of being a part of something that was . . . well, something that maybe we could write about someday. If we didn't know what was happening, man, how could we write about it? That was our story, and we were sticking to it.

Let me insert here, for the record, that this book is strictly my story, what I saw and heard, how it sounded to my ears and appeared in my eyes—a very personal view of a bunch of young, ambitious, intelligent and adventuresome people who made their living at their typewriters or musical instruments.

People who shared similar viewpoints on a number of things and mutually participated in some days and nights of tiptoeing along edges. There were few rules, if any. Those rules that existed were usually unwritten—even unspoken, although some were occasionally spoken, such as "A Poonzar never takes off his costume until he's done his act." And "Everything that is not a mystery is guesswork."

Nor is this book a critique of the works by prose and song writers discussed here. I read a lot, but I haven't read all those books Larry McMurtry once said one must read in order to argue with him. I'll take his word for it, on one level, that it's probably true Texas hasn't yet produced even one really great book. Certainly, it hasn't yet produced even one Faulkner; only Mississippi has done that.

What Texas did produce, beginning in the 1960s, was a rabble of writers, including songwriters, who had the courage (gall?) to step up to the plate at a time when being a serious writer from Texas wasn't totally unheard of, but was so seldom heard of there was a dearth of role models for young Texans coming up who believed they could write. Those few who had written serious fiction with some success, as often as not either wrote Westerns or tried to disassociate themselves from Texas. (See Katherine Ann Porter, for instance.) This wild bunch from the sixties not only didn't disassociate themselves from modern times in the Lone Star State, they set most of their stories there. Sometimes they were even accused of being Professional Texans, heaven forbid. In point of fact, you could say with confidence that they blazed a trail for Texans who came along later and dared to write about today's Texas.

Notice that I called this particular group of Texans a "rabble." It was the word I finally settled on after perusing page 87 in my *Roget's Pocket Thesaurus* under the word "group."

I knew "group" wasn't the right word to encapsulate this particular . . . well, rabble of writers, but couldn't come up with a really accurate synonym, even after getting help from Roget.

Nor was this the first time I had searched more or less in vain for the right word for these writers who headquartered in Texas and mostly maintained themselves by newspapering, before books, movies and magazines began contributing significantly to their livelihoods. The first time was back in the latter part of 1964. I was in Washington, D.C., for a few months. (I had gone there to surrender, thinking that would be where you would go to do such as that. But I never could locate the place where you surrendered; so, I wound up back in Texas after a few months.) I had sold a piece to *Sports Illustrated*—with the help of Bud Shrake and Dan Jenkins, who were working there then and rode the train up to Manhattan to discuss revisions. While there, I had lunch with Margaret Cousins, a native Texan (from Munday) who had been editor of *Good Housekeeping* for a long time and, when we had lunch, was working as a senior editor at Doubleday.

She surprised me by saying Texas seemed to be growing itself a "school of writers." Or maybe she said "accumulating" or "developing." Something along those lines, anyway. She even compared this "Texas School" to what was going on in Chicago back in the twenties and thirties when Ben Hecht and Charles MacArthur and Carl Sandburg and others were raising cane at and around Chicago newspapers and writing some pretty good stuff on the side. She mentioned Shrake, Jenkins and Brammer, and even me, as the present-day Texas counterparts of Chicago's Hecht, et al.

I told Cousins she had failed to mention the strangest of all the new bunch of Texas writers—namely, Larry McMurtry, who had already finished his second novel, *Leaving Cheyenne*, that was so finely honed, with such an authentic West Texas voice, that at least two of his writer friends cried over a long distance phone call, because they hadn't written it. McMurtry wandered through Austin now and then in the sixties, usually staying with Brammer. He never stayed long, however, because it was too hard to stick to his rigid schedule of writing (at least four hours, daily, seven days a week) with all the interruptions by Brammer's constant stream of fans, friends and hangers-on showing up at all hours.

Then there was Larry L. King, expatriate Texan from the Midland area, who had flipped a vital switch and given up a well-paying (with benefits) job in Congressman Jim Wright's Washington office to become a "full-time" writer. King's first novel, *The One-Eyed Man*, was due out soon.

I'm not certain just when Maddog, Inc. was officially formed. The date doesn't matter, since the actual formation of the club with a name and slogan: "Doing indefinable services to mankind" is more or less beside the point. Way back in the early 1960s Maddog members—years before there was a Maddog, Inc.—were gathering at the flimsiest excuse in Dallas, Fort Worth or, more than likely, Austin, to make merry and wait for something wonderful and unique to happen. As far as I know, something wonderful and unique never happened at one of those gatherings, but I wasn't there for all of them. And, more important, hope springs eternal and all that.

Bud Shrake and Gary Cartwright, when they were sports page columnists for the Dallas dailies, usually roomed together when they had left their wives for this or that reason. It was said by some that, when Shrake and his wife, Joyce, broke up and Shrake would get an apartment, Cartwright would find a reason to leave Barbara so he could join Shrake at his new party headquarters.

At those early parties, Bud and Jap (as most of his friends affectionately called Cartwright) could usually be talked into performing an opera or two, making up the lyrics as they went along. They were amazingly good at this—at least to my untrained and perhaps biased ears. Once—at least once that I know of personally—two Dallas policemen showed up at the door of their apartment during a rather noisy costume party and were awarded first prize for best costumes.

In those early Maddog days (and nights), Billie Lee Brammer and I were the only ones with a book already published, except for Larry McMurtry, who more often than not didn't make it to our party gatherings. (Someone pointed out that this was no doubt a major reason McMurtry finished his second novel so far ahead of everybody else.)

In McMurtry's absence, Billie Lee and I, therefore, were usually the only "famous arthers" in attendance, and I am afraid we made the most of it from time to time. Like the night in Austin when a nice matron type walked up to me and gushed, "You're the first famous arther I've ever met in person. Would you say something profound to me, personally so I can tell my friends about it?"

It never occurred to me she could be serious, so I replied, "Hmm . . . well, I was just looking around and thinking, 'We're all running around like chickens with our heads cut off.'" But she was serious, and my profundity made her clap her hands and cry "Ooooo! I know exactly what you mean . . . 'We're all running around like chickens with our heads chopped off!'" And off she went to spread the news.

Fletcher Boone, an Austin artist, and Brammer were standing nearby and heard this exchange. "Don't count your chickens before they hatch," Boone inserted. "It's lucky," Brammer added, "that every cloud has a silver lining."

And it went on like this the rest of the evening, with each Maddog adding his or her own cliché contribution. We soon discovered, to our increasing exasperation, we couldn't say anything without adding or inserting a cliché. It was noon the next day before we shook it off.

Then there was the time at a party in Fort Worth thrown by some of my more mainstream friends. I showed up, but was so under the weather I was avoiding contact with other guests. I didn't feel like talking to anybody, so I wandered out onto the patio and sat in a swing and stared at nothing until a nice lady wandered out and sat beside me. I don't remember what she talked about, but I do remember that she talked a lot. I nodded occasionally and maybe grunted a time or two. After what seemed to me a long time, one of our hosts wandered out and asked the nice lady if she had enjoyed conversing with "our famous arther"; and she gushed, "I've just had the most interesting conversation of my entire life!"

I pondered that for some time; still do occasionally.

I feel I must point out here, for the record, that you are either a Maddog or you're not. There are no specific requirements listed anywhere. Those who are already card-carrying members simply identify those who are naturally Maddogs, but who haven't yet been "handed the card." Usually, it is considered proper for a Maddog who believes he has discovered an uncarded Maddog to seek confirmation from another card-carrying member, if it is convenient. For instance, at an Austin gathering in the seventies, I pointed out to Shrake and Cartwright that singer/songwriter Billy Joe Shaver was an uncarded Maddog, and Cartwright decided to check him out. Shrake and I watched as Jap approached Billy Joe and engaged him in conversation we couldn't hear from where we stood. Soon, Jap returned to our huddle and nodded. "He's one all right," he said. We asked what had convinced him and he said Billy Joe had drawn a happy face on the stump of a finger he'd lost in a rodeo accident and showed it to Jap proudly, saying, "Some folks will do anything for morphine."

• • •

"Have you noticed," asked Gary Cartwright, surveying the people in the Driskill Hotel bar back in the fall of 1987, "that we all look ten years younger?"

King scratched his beard, which was somewhat grayer than the last time I'd seen it, and replied, "I was thinking the same thing."

We all nodded our agreement and continued to sip our Diet Cokes during the following moments of silence.

The real question before the house, although it was never articulated, was: "What are we going to do now that we are together again and it is still the shank of the evening?"

"We've already missed *Wheel of Fortune*," noted one grizzled veteran Maddog.

Nobody commented on that. We were waiting for Susan Walker to show up and tell us what to do.

IN the Days
Before MAdDOgS

A Little Background Music, Please

There I was, driving triumphantly toward my old home town of Lubbock for the first time in fifteen years, rakishly spinning along in my snazzy little Triumph convertible, headed for a book-signing party where I was to be the guest of honor and autograph copies of my just-published novel.

I stopped just outside the city limits to take down the top on the car. The rain didn't start until I was almost through downtown Lubbock, as I searched, in vain, for someone, anyone, who might recognize me. During those fifteen years I had been away, I'd accomplished some interesting things: I had done my stint in the U. S. Navy during The Big War. Coached a championship high school football team. Worked a hitch as managing editor of Hodding Carter's energetic little daily in the Mississippi Delta town of Greenville during the years immediately following the U. S. Supreme Court's ruling that separate schools were not equal. And there was my novel that had recently been published. The famous author's triumphant return scenario didn't play out altogether perfectly, but nonetheless, moments from that day are indelibly etched in my memory and to this day, I still enjoy an occasional satisfying flashback.

The way I figured it, we were in the fourth wave of pioneers in the Texas panhandle country, my family and I. Unless you count dinosaurs and varmints, which I'm not. I am counting Indians. I've always had a thing about Indians. Native Americans. In our neighborhood, kids used to play cowboys and Indians a lot, and I usually got first dubs on being an Indian. Being cast as cowboy was not particularly fascinating to me and some of my boyhood West Texas playmates. There was something mysteriously appealing about Indians to many of us back then, and I'm only somewhat reluctant to admit that for me, there still is to this day. I was particularly fascinated by tales of the Comanches, who had wandered the prairies where I grew up merely a brief decade or two before my family and I, and nearly all of our neighbors, arrived at that remote and windswept place.

An unlikely number of us growing up on the High Plains in those days claimed to have Indian blood flowing in our veins, even though none of us had any empirical data to back up those claims. I didn't, anyhow, and I was one of the more tenacious claimants, but I doubt many of my pigeon-toe walking comrades had any more authentic claims to Indian blood than I had.

My father moved us out there in about 1928. Quanah Parker, the half-white Comanche chief, and his legendary young warriors, in the late 1800s, were outsmarting the pony soldiers not far from the place where we settled. The Comanches were a nomadic people and left few signs behind on the lean and lonesome land that they ever passed that way.

Long before the Indians passed through that region, sixteenth-century Spanish soldier-explorers searched there for the mythical Lost Cities of Gold. They trudged across a prairie bereft of landmarks. To mark their trail, they drove wooden stakes in the earth to guide them back to Mexico. The Spanish christened the seemingly desolate land, El Llano Estacado—the Staked Plains. That name is used out there yet, and proudly, four hundred years later. A soldier in Francisco Coronado's expedition kept a rudimentary journal of their pilgrimage. It was the first book written about Texas, they say. Because of the explorer-soldier's journal documenting the ancient Spanish exploration—crumbling fragments of the only written record of the legendary expedition to survive and be handed down through the centuries—we learned about Coronado and others in our Texas history classes at school.

In Lubbock, when I was growing up there, Mexican kids, some of whom were descendants, perhaps, of those long-departed Spanish soldiers, had to go to the "Meskin" School and live in "Meskin Town." Some white teenage boys who were (I'm ashamed to admit) boys I looked up to—my athletic heroes—occasionally rode through Meskin Town in their daddies' cars, bombarding the dark-skinned inhabitants with day-old bakery pies. As far as I know, there were no retaliatory raids by Mexican teens. I suppose this illustrates rather picturesquely how times have changed, even while remaining the same.

Children of local Spanish (as opposed to Meskin) families could attend "our" schools, and several did. Spanish families had money and Meskin families were very poor. That's how you could distinguish one from the other. Consuelo, one of the prettiest girls at Lubbock High, was Spanish. She did not live in Meskin Town.

Following the European explorers' march across the High Plains—during which they lost a few ponies that turned out to be the ancestors of those the Indians would later master— a few centuries went by before any other two-legged invaders bothered to seriously explore that daunting region. I suppose various tribes and klatches of Indians passed through on their way to better places. Maybe they even spent a little time at this or that narrow trickle of water etching its way through the enormous rocky canyons. But apparently, nobody ever stayed there longer than they had to, until Quanah Parker and his Comanche juvenile delinquents escaped from the Oklahoma reservation and took advantage of the magnificent arid vastness and the apparent scarcity of food sources to be found there to shield themselves from their enemies. Soldiers couldn't sneak up on them in a surprise assault there on the High Plains. It was too flat. There was no foliage, no hills, for would-be marauders to hide behind, and only Quanah and his band knew where the rare water holes were to be found. Quanah himself was never really defeated by the United States military. In the end, he negotiated his peace and later rode, wearing his splendid tribal regalia, in an inaugural parade in Washington, D.C. The hard country was Quanah's ally. He and his braves learned to use it. The soldiers tried to vanquish it.

After the Indians finally left, the next surge of High Plains invaders was led by cattle ranchers. It took at least ten wiry acres of grassland to support a single cow, so the cowboys and their animals spread out and didn't crowd up the place much. Then, just ahead of my family, came the farmers, the sodbusters.

That reminds me of a story I heard in Mississippi one time, long after I had left the Plains. It was meant to put high fallutin' Mississippians in their place and it went something like this: The few real aristocrats who came to America from Europe remained in Virginia and prospered. Those early Virginians who for one reason or other couldn't make it there, moved west into Georgia and the Carolinas. Those who couldn't succeed there, moved farther west into Alabama, Tennessee, Mississippi, Arkansas and Louisiana. If they couldn't cut the mustard in any of those places, or if they were running from the law, they ended up in Texas.

To carry that a step further: those who couldn't make the grade in the more plush and fertile climes of East and Central Texas pushed on into far West Texas and eventually they came upon the raw-boned wide open spaces of the High Plains— the Llano Estacado. It's an insight into the Texas mentality, incidentally, to discover that not only are Texans not the least bit ashamed of that somewhat disreputable heritage—they are damn proud of it.

Driving west from Fort Worth on Highway 82, past Archer City, Olney, Guthrie, and through the grasslands and the deep red ravines and gullies of the gigantic ranches—the Pitchfork, the 6666, and the Beggs Cattle Company—you come upon a sudden rise in the road. My ears always pop when I drive up that incline as it takes me up five or six hundred feet above sea level in less than a mile. At the top of this rise, the land flattens outrageously, stretching clear to the foothills of the New Mexico mountains. I used to try and imagine what thoughts must have blown through the minds of the first settlers who came that way in their covered wagons, when first they climbed that sharp incline to scout out what was on the top and were abruptly confronted by those endless miles of endless miles on the other side. I can almost hear the windburnt man of the family shouting back down the incline to his wife, "Hey, Maude, you ain't gonna believe this! There's nothin' up here but nothin'!"

Small wonder it took so long for the sodbusters and cattle ranchers to be motivated to settle those vast empty plains stretching to nowhere.

I started to school in Hart Camp on The Great American Desert, as the land out there was still labeled on maps of the United States not many years before we moved out there to seek my daddy's fortune. I fell in love for the first time there— with my first grade teacher, Miss Gipson, who roomed at our house because there were no other houses within walking distance of the school, which (oh! happy day!) was just across the road from our house and the cotton gin. Miss Gipson is still beautiful and kind in my memory.

One day she ventured outside during recess. To impress her, I took a running dive, head-first, down the big slide and skinned my hands painfully on the sharp-edged caliche rocks that covered the school yard. Years later, I recalled this childhood episode to my mother, who smiled and commented that it seemed to her I had been doing that same thing over and over ever since. (Sometimes that soft-spoken woman could surprise me.)

Mother was nineteen when she and Daddy left East Texas and headed west. She had never been out of Angelina County. Not many of the roads out of the piney woods were paved, and just before Mother and Daddy reached the town of Forney—now a suburb of Dallas—their Ford roadster got stuck so badly my father had to struggle through the mud to a nearby farmhouse and hire the farmer and his mules to pull them out. The happy farmer was pulling out another muddy car mired in the muck as they drove away. Mother has told me many times that when she and Daddy left the family farm near Lufkin, her father, a stern lay preacher, as well as farmer and carpenter, told her he was certain he would never see her again in this lifetime.

In Cotton Center and Hart Camp, Mother cooked and cleaned, sewed all the family's clothes, and washed the laundry by hand on a scrub board. Sometimes in winter, when she hung the wash out to dry on the line behind the house, it was frozen stiff by the time she got the clothespins in place. Summers, as often as not, the blowing sand made it necessary for her to take the laundry down off the line and scrub everything all over again. Many of the women living out there in those harsh times were driven mad by the loneliness, the relentless wind.

Mother cooked for the gin hands and often added their dirty clothes to our family wash. She ironed everything, even the sheets. Mother sometimes grumbled about how the sand always seemed to find its way into her house and cover everything, no matter how often she dusted and swept and mopped. That's the only complaint I ever heard from her.

We moved out there when the Farm Bureau hired Daddy to build cotton gins and operate them. Somebody had gotten the bright idea that cotton could be grown and harvested in fields as flat as table tops easier than it could on rolling or swampy, or any other kind of fields. And they were right. Last I heard, that region of Texas was still the number one cotton producer in America.

My father learned about cotton gins and ginning cotton from his father in deep East Texas, where the forest land had to be cleared of pine trees and brush before cotton could be grown and harvested. But they seldom had to worry about getting enough rain. It sometimes rained too much and at the wrong times in East Texas, but droughts were rare.

My earliest memories are set in Cotton Center, where there was only the gin my father had built, our house and a general store. If there were any other buildings, I don't remember them. You could see for miles in every direction. The Texas Panhandle is not overrun with people today, but it was even more sparsely populated back then. The biggest nearby town was Plainview, perched on the highway connecting Lubbock and Amarillo. Cotton Center was several miles west of that highway and south of Plainview. Daddy and his truck driver, an amiable man everybody called "Brub," often cut across the prairie, ignoring the roads, when they needed to drive to Plainview in a hurry. There was nothing to speak of in the way.

The family migrated to a nearby crossroads community called Hart Camp when I was about six or seven. My father built another gin there. Mother used to fry up baskets of hamburgers, and I would take them to the gin where farmers were lined up for what, to me, seemed like a mile, waiting—sometimes all night—for their turn to have their wagonloads of cotton sucked up through the long pipe into the belly of the gin where the sharp bolls and seeds were separated from the soft cotton that was then bound into bales weighing several hundred pounds each, for easy hauling to market. The first thing I remember wanting to be when I grew up was the operator of the huge suction pipe that emptied those wagons of raw cotton. We sold those hamburgers for a nickel apiece, and a full basket never lasted more than a few minutes among those hungry cotton farmers.

I remember there being a lot of snow back then, and it wasn't just because I was little. One winter in Cotton Center, snow piled against one side of our house all the way to the roof. We still have photographs to prove that memory. From those Cotton Center and Hart Camp days, I remember the fearsome thrill of crawling along the high, narrow rafters in the vast emptiness of the gin during the off season. I'll never forget one time being deathly ill after chewing castor beans at the urging of my cousin James, who was always doing stuff like that.

I recall a lot of people and images from those long ago times. But I don't remember ever seeing a single book (other than the Bible, of course) in any of the houses we lived in. Nor in any of the houses of friends and relatives we visited. Recalling this bit of Texas cultural trivia reminds me that years later, after I left Texas, when I was a young man working at a newspaper in the Mississippi delta, I was surprised to discover that many delta farmers, in that poorest of states, did have books in their homes. Some owned many books, and some even sent their sons to Ivy League colleges. Princeton was a favorite. (In later years, the planters would send their daughters to excellent institutions of higher learning as well as their sons.) Not that those delta plantation owners were entirely civilized in all the best ways. Many were terrible racists. But there was, in that rural society, an abiding respect for education—at least relatively so, compared with the typical farming community in West Texas when I was growing up.

Even today, it seems to me that some Texans remain suspicious of "too much education." That's generalizing, I know. But it's well-documented that the Lone Star State, even in boom times, has never come down strong on the side of better education. Could this be because our forefathers were so far removed from "aristocratic" Virginia? I don't know the answer to that. But I do know that many people I was familiar with, as a child and very young man in West Texas, had a great many admirable traits, but respect for a broad education and a love of literature were not among them.

Thanks in large part to J. Frank Dobie and his friend, Walter Prescott Webb, however, many Texans of a certain vintage have long been fascinated by their state's history and folklore. The Texas Folklore Society, one of Dobie's early projects, is still active and flourishing. Until a relatively short time ago, Dobie, Webb and Roy Bedichek, the naturalist, were the best-known Texas writers. Katherine Anne Porter may have been more famous abroad, but she seemed to dodge being identified as a Texan.

Stanley Walker, the Texan who became one of the legendary city editors of the *New York Herald Tribune* in that grand old daily's heyday and, later as a chronicler of Texas and things Texan in a series of books, once wrote that his friend Dobie, "folklorist, historian, journalist and former teacher, was the man who did more than any other person to make Texans aware of the richness of their history and environment." Walker added that Dobie owed much of his reputation to the recognition of outsiders. "In Boston, New York and England (Dobie) is something of a figure. In Texas, he has many friends, but there are those who think of him as merely 'that fellow the University had to fire because he was too radical.'" Then Walker added: "It is almost impossible to believe, but it is a fact that a very rich man once confided to me the severity of his objection to Dobie: 'He's too close to that Greek, Socrates.'"

My family moved to Lubbock from Hart Camp when I was in the second grade—supposed to be in the second grade, that is. Because I had attended first grade at a small country school, the Lubbock school authorities saw fit to move me back one grade; so I was a first-grader again. But only for a short time. Once they observed the depth of my intellectual acumen, they moved me up to my rightful place—the second grade.

This was at K. Carter Elementary School. One of my first close human encounters there was with a bully type who, for reasons beyond my abilities to comprehend, got his jollies out of knocking my books from my arms onto the floor each and every time he walked past me in the halls. This continued until a burr-headed, bare-footed hero named Tuffy Nabors told the bully to "Lay Off!" Or words that effect. Which the big bully did immediately and forever, and young Tuffy became my first real friend in the big city of Lubbock.

It was Tuffy Nabors who gave me my first and only nickname—"Killer Diller." He coined the name the day I pitched on a playground softball team and managed to whack five batters in a row during recess at K. Carter Elementary School in Lubbock. I wasn't proud of the way I got it, but I was, nevertheless, pleased with the sound of my new nickname. Killer Diller. It took on several macho connotations in my young mind. I tried to keep the nickname for years afterwards, but my friends wouldn't cooperate. Even in high school, as a sophomore, I signed yearbooks, "Killer Diller Milner," but to no avail. Everybody still called me "J. D." I never liked being only initials. It seemed bland and bloodless. Finally, in the Navy during World War II, I called myself "Jay." Not as dashing as Killer Diller, I reasoned, but decidedly more so than "J. D." Some of my closest friends—oldest friends, I should say— still call me "J. D." Funny, but it doesn't seem important any more. The "J," incidentally, doesn't stand for anything. On my birth certificate it's just "J." I've gradually come to moderately admire the name my "D" stands for—Dunston. When I was a kid, I hated it. Sounded sissy. Now it sounds dignified, somehow.

Big Daddy
and Me

Some of you may remember a magnificent professional football player known as Big Daddy Lipscomb. He was all-everything as a pro defensive tackle, and, for his time, a physical giant. By "for his time," I mean when he was playing. I've forgotten exactly when that was, but it was either in the 1950s or the 1960s, or both. He may have overlapped into the 1970s. But that's beside the point—or I would look it up. The point is that Big Daddy Lipscomb was an admirable athlete and somewhat of a hero of mine, for several reasons. Besides being a big man, he was sharp and shrewd enough to manhandle the giants opposite him, and perhaps more importantly, he was an outspoken leader, on and off the field.

So, you might imagine my surprise and even puzzlement— at first, anyway—to read—in *Esquire*, I think it was—soon after his death at a relatively young age, but several years after his retirement from pro football, that Big Daddy once told a reporter, "You probably can't tell by looking, but I've been scared all my life."

Those words were printed in bold face beneath a full-page impressionistic portrait of Big Daddy, preceding a long article about him.

My first reaction was something like: Naaah. Surely the man was not afraid of anything! Not generically afraid, certainly! Then I thought: Surely Big Daddy wouldn't lie about something like that! It took great courage, actually, for him to admit it—a famous pro football star whose macho image was a vital stratagem of his game. This was no Fancy Dan wide receiver or quarterback. This was a hardened defensive lineman! This was Big Daddy Lipscomb.

I played in the line in high school and college just like Big Daddy. Well, not *just* like Big Daddy, but you know what I mean. I remember being scared as I stood on the field waiting for the kickoff before each game. I would actually consider walking off the field and telling the coach "I quit." Or telling him I had to go to the bathroom and just keep on walking—run home to Mama. Of course, I never did, and soon the ball was flying toward us or toward the other team, and somebody hit me or I hit somebody, and the fear disappeared. Not just momentarily flying out of my mind—but gone, as if it had never been there at all. And I wouldn't even think of it again until the next game as I stood waiting for another opening kickoff.

In those ancient seasons, there was no such thing as a specialist—no special teams who did nothing but play on kickoffs and punts and passing downs and stuff like that. We played, not just both ways, but every way—because if you came out of the game, you couldn't go back in until the next quarter. These days, as I watch multimillionaire pro football players on TV, I wonder about them. Those special teams guys who don't do anything but play on kickoffs, do they experience the same dread—fright—that I did in my day?

Over the years, I've thought about Big Daddy's startling statement about being fearful all his life, and somehow I just knew that kickoff anxiety wasn't the fear he was talking about. He may have experienced that anxiety, too—I think most football players do, or did before the special teams system became a vital part of the game. But what Big Daddy said about being scared sounded to me more like he meant *off*, rather than *on* the field.

And that made me think—made me take a hard look at my own anxieties. And they were there. You probably can't tell by looking, I thought to myself, but I've been scared most of my life. Way back, in the darkest alleys of my mind, there always lurked a dread or uneasiness that added up to fear. Not any specific fear like, "I'm terrified of big barking dogs that run at me!" Or, "I'm afraid to bungee jump!" Or, "I'm really scared when a cop car signals me to pull over." Not the kind of fear that jumps out at you and shouts, "Boo!" But rather a kind of fear that I could hide from most of the time, as it crouched back there in the darkness, keeping me from reaching my full potential.

I had no idea of the source of my fearfulness, or any explanation for it. They say all fear is fear of the unknown. That makes sense. The kind of fear—or whatever it was—that caused me to want to run off the field as I waited for game-opening kickoffs probably did stem from not knowing what was in store for me in the immediate minutes ahead. Would some big old boy on the other team knock my head off? Break my bones? Make me look so silly the coach would yell at me in front of the whole team? That kind of fear.

But the real fear—the dread that constantly lurked in the unlit recesses of my mind—where did that come from? I contemplated those enigmatic anxieties a lot, wondering what might have happened in my early life to cause it—telling myself that it didn't make any sense. I'd always done pretty well at everything I'd tried as an adolescent—no bleak puberty, no troublesome teen years—and throughout adulthood. So what did I have to fear?

I was certain it wasn't genetic. My mama wasn't afraid of anything even though she probably should have been, especially after marrying my rambling father and joining his family. Mother had grown up in a small town and on a farm outside of an even smaller town. (Oh yeah, I remember she was afraid of cows and other farm animals, so her chores were always in the house, or in the back yard boiling the family's wash in one of those large pots over an open fire.) She never finished school and I'm convinced she was dyslexic way back before dyslexia was cool.

Her father, William Rushing Sanders, was a man of stern convictions, a lay preacher who didn't stand for any foolishness, as people used to say in praise of strict parents. Mother's mother, Nellie Tanner Sanders, was quietly intractable. When her husband died (I was only about three years old, so I don't really remember him), Grandma Sanders became the head of the large extended family, including a number of cousins and the widows of two sons who died young and all their children. Things apparently went along very much as they always had when Grandpa Sanders was alive. Grace was said at the table and the Bible was the only book in the house. All the family's major historical events were recorded there. And if someone needed a bed for a night, or a month, they came to Grandma Sanders's house.

But after my mother's marriage to John Milner, her life was altered—rather drastically—forever. "John's family talked terrible," she told me many years after the fact. "I had never heard anybody talk like that before in my life. One day John and Jim (Daddy's twin brother) went to town and it was al-

most dark when Jim came home by hisself, and I asked him
where John was, and he said he'd stopped at that old barn to
take a crap. 'Well,' I said, 'that's one thing he's going to have to
stop doing now that we're married.' I thought he meant he
was shooting dice."

The Milners were, in the vernacular of the time and place,
relatively "well fixed" financially. Grandpa Milner was something of a mechanical wizard when it came to cotton gins. He
owned a gin and had invented something that made ginning
cotton easier or better or swifter or something but, (as the
family legend goes), he let somebody steal it because he never
got around to filing for a patent.

"Mrs. Milner was the strong one in that family," mother
always declared. "When she died, Mr. Milner started drinking
and the kids sold the gin and they all (three boys and three
girls and Grandpa) moved to Colorado Springs, Colorado, and
stayed there, living it up, until they spent all the money."

Mother worked from just a few weeks after I was born
until she was eighty. "I don't know how I did it," she told me
many times after her retirement. "I didn't know anything,
but I was never scared. I guess I didn't have enough sense to
be scared. I never applied for a job I didn't get."

She'd made the complete circle when she retired in Lufkin
from her job selling women's better dresses at Clark's, the
"best store in town." When she lived in Fort Worth, she sold
ladies fashions at Neiman-Marcus.

Since I've known her, mother's main interests have been
her children: my younger brother Wilbur Ray, and my sister
Marieta Don, and of course, me. She outlived both my brother
and sister. She had what you might call a two-track mind—
her work and her children. The rest of the world was just out
there doing whatever it did and, unless it was something earth-
shaking, such as the assassination of President John F.

Kennedy, she pretty much let it slide by without trying to figure out what it meant. So after she retired and started watching television, she was shocked and appalled and not a little bit fearful. According to what she saw on the TV screen, the world was falling apart, coming to an end, just like the Bible said. I tried to explain that her shock resulted from suddenly seeing everything bad that happened everywhere in the world almost as soon as it happened.

"People have been killing each other and starving each other and stealing from each other and raping and pillaging since way before the time of Jesus," I reassured her. "We just didn't know about all of it before TV came along and sent people out searching for disasters to throw it right into our faces several times a day. Nobody loves a disaster like television. Newspapers have always taken notice of calamitous happenings, too, but you could ignore those stories if you wanted to, and just turn to the sports page or the funnies, or whatever. But TV news won't let you ignore it, especially if it's something really horrible. They set us up for it. They whet our appetites for it all day before their news programs, then show us pictures of it—in color. And the gorier the better."

After I had run through one of my lectures about how the world has always had bad people doing bad things, and we just had not been burdened by having to learn about it all at once every day until television came along, she would get one of those looks on her face like she used to get when I was a kid and tried to tell her I hadn't eaten all the cookies in the cookie jar, when she knew I had and I knew she knew. I don't believe I ever convinced her that the world was no worse off now than it had ever been. She had proof—right there before her eyes. Who could argue with that?

TV commercials often puzzled her, as well. Once she asked me how much it cost to put an advertisement on television. I wasn't sure, but guessed it was thousands of dollars for network commercials and went on to tell her that one minute commercials during the Super Bowl cost many thousands. A double mint gum commercial came on about that time.

"Do they sell enough chewing gum to pay for that?" she asked. I've wondered about that myself from time to time ever since.

Secret Urges

One day during study hall, (when I was in the seventh grade I think), I was browsing and musing in the library stacks and ran across the Jack London novel, *White Fang*. I no longer remember what it was that attracted me to it, but I checked it out and took it home and read it. What an impression London's story made on my young mind! I read it at least three times before the year was out and read *Call of the Wild* and every other Jack London book I could find. When I had run out of London books, I was moved to read books by other writers and eventually wound up the avid reader I am to this day.

The pleasure of reading books was not one I remember sharing with my high school friends, male or female, although some of them may have been secret readers like I was. I know Franklin Butler, who played guard on the varsity, used to recite "The Face on the Barroom Floor" and other poems, including, in the Olde English, long pieces from Chaucer's *Canterbury Tales*, when we were riding the bus home from a football game we had won. (When we lost, hardly a word was spoken all the way home.)

Lubbock was not famous for producing a lot of serious writers. I remember in 1961, on my triumphant return to autograph copies of my newly published novel, I visited Lubbock High and Mrs. Grove, who was still the librarian there. She showed me a corner shelf that held only three books— mine and two by Frank X. Tolbert, who also had attended school there awhile. "This is a shelf I've reserved for books by Lubbock authors," she said.

● ● ●

I don't know where they came from but I had secret urges to write as far back as my junior high years. They might have been inspired by my love for Jack London's novels, or the fact that one of my English teachers (Miss Honey was her name, and she really was one) liked the essays I wrote for her classes.

The only classmate who encouraged me to write was a pretty brunette named Grace Halsell. Grace was editor of the junior high student newspaper, and I wrote a couple of pieces for her before I got up the courage to come out for football. After that, I had no time for anything but worrying about whether or not I would ever weigh more than a hundred pounds. See, I was small—but I was slow. Adding some weight seemed to be my only hope, since I seriously doubted I would ever gain a lot more running speed, and I was right. I still remember the look of, well, what I interpreted at that time as a mixture of disdain and pity on young Grace Halsell's wise-beyond-her-years eyes when we passed in the halls after I launched my career as a jock.

I was also a secret fan of country music. The hep (that's what the word was back then) kids I admired were fans of Big Band music—Glen Miller, Tommy and Jimmy Dorsey, and others like them. They sneered at what was then called "hill-billy" music. I liked Big Bands, too, but my real favorites were Roy Acuff, Little Jimmy Dickens, Ernest Tubb, Bob Wills and the Light Crust Dough Boys, and others who broadcast out of Nashville and Fort Worth. But that kind of music was regarded as hicky—too country (too close to home), so I never mentioned my love for it to my hep friends and listened to it over the radio in secret only in the privacy of my own inner sanctum.

My friends on the football team were less than encouraging concerning this strange new desire of mine to pursue writing for fun. Even in high school after we had all gotten to know each other better, my friends and teammates quashed my writing efforts. I spent a great deal of time at home for several nights composing a skit, planning starring roles for several of my football-playing buddies and myself. When I showed them the script and suggested that we rehearse the act and volunteer to perform at an assembly program, they hoohawed as if they thought I'd lost my mind. Years later, at a reunion gathering, they denied this, claiming not to recall anything of the sort.

Grace Halsell went on to become something of a famous author. She worked as a reporter on newspapers in Fort Worth, New York and Tokyo, and published several books. For a time, she worked as a speech writer for President Lyndon Johnson.

In the late 1950s, in my job as assistant to the editor of the editorial page of the *New York Herald Tribune*, one of my duties was to handle columns they recruited from our own people working in various *Tribune* bureaus and others around the country. One day I found in my office mail an article submitted from Lima, Peru, by Grace Halsell, profiling the American wife of the president of Peru. Grace knew the *Herald Tribune* was buying unsolicited pieces, but had no idea her old Lubbock classmate was in charge of selecting those that would be printed. We used two of her pieces.

I was not the least bit surprised to see that Grace Halsell was an accomplished writer. She came to New York shortly after that and we managed to spend a brief, rather awkward, evening together. It was sometime later that Halsell consulted a dermatologist at Yale about a drug to turn her skin dark. Then she spent six months in the Virgin Islands getting a deep tan as the sun worked with the drug to darken her skin. Then, wearing black contact lenses, she spent time in Harlem and Mississippi as a black woman and wrote a book about her experiences on the other side of the color line. The book, *Soul Sister*, was a bestseller. Books that followed were *Bessie Yellowhair*, about life as a Navajo Indian; *The Illegals*, about her adventures with illegal aliens sneaking across the Texas-Mexico border with no identification; *Los Viejos* about a group of people in South America, some of whom lived to be over one hundred years of age; and two books about the Middle East—*Journey to Jerusalem* and *Prophecy and Politics: Militant Evangelists on the Road to Nuclear War*. If there are still Lubbock Writers shelves in the Library of Lubbock High School, I am sure Grace Halsell's books can be found residing there.

Hodding Carter, A Damn Good Reporter

Neither God nor lawful man discriminates between races when the taking of life or the breaking of the lesser laws of mankind are involved. Think on that, you people who profess to be Christian or democratic or fair. Until we in Mississippi look upon law and crime without relation to the color or faith or nationality of the principals, we have no right to lift our heads and ask for equal treatment in the concert of states or the community of nations.

Hodding Carter, *Delta Democrat-Times*
Greenville, Mississippi—1953

During the first thirty or so years of my life I tried hard to conform, but they kept changing the Rules. Or so it seemed to me. My view of the proper lifestyle, my social and political attitudes, were shaped to a large extent by my teachers and coaches. They seemed sincere in their beliefs, and I took them seriously. The questions came later, after I was gone from the High Plains, and got to know some of our business and political leaders at closer range. Some of the best people I met were newspaper editors.

Looking back over my life in recent years, I have decided I must spring from roots deep in the British and Scottish service traditions. I have always felt this otherwise unexplained need—a need so deeply ingrained in my psyche it had to be instinctive, rather than cerebral—that I should make my living doing something useful to the community, or some segment of the community, the whole state, or the world—the larger the segment, the better. To be worthy of the space I occupied and the air I breathed, I felt I ought to be a coach, or a lawyer, or a doctor, or even a minister. After I had been associated with Andy Harmon and his staff for a time, I came to believe Journalism (capital "J") was an honorable calling—on a par with lawyering and doctoring, and, yes—even preaching and coaching.

Locally-owned, independent-thinking daily newspapers were once the real backbone of this nation's freedom. Unfortunately, all over the country, chains are gobbling up small, medium and large dailies and have been doing so for some time. Last report I saw said that the chains control more than eighty percent of the nation's daily newspaper circulation.

I have been lucky enough to work for three of the best medium-sized daily newspapers in the country—the *American* in Hattiesburg, Mississippi, before it was sold to a chain; the *Delta Democrat-Times* in Greenville, Mississippi before it was sold to a chain; and the *Daily News* in Lufkin, Texas, before and after the Cox chain bought it. Two of those dailies—the one in Greenville and the one in Lufkin—were Pulitzer Prize winners before they succumbed to offers by chains.

I've worked for and around newspapers of just about all sizes in my checkered career as a journalist and teacher, and I have never known of a successful newspaper or magazine (as I gauge success) whose controlling editor didn't have a crazy streak in him (or her). Henry Luce, the founding genius of Time, Inc., is one famous case in point. Harold Ross of the *New Yorker* is another on the national level. Andy Harmon, Hodding Carter the Elder, and Joe Murray are outstanding models on the local, small to medium size daily newspaper level. Mr. Harmon and the senior Carter are no longer in this earthly realm, but in their day, each boasted decidedly demented characteristics and they put out lively local newspapers. Joe Murray, the last I heard, is still among us, and still going strong although he now writes a nationally syndicated column. As editor of the Lufkin, Texas, *Daily News* he won a Pulitzer and, as his many friends and foes will tell you without hesitation, he has a crazy streak a yard wide. I rest my case.

I began my career as a daily newspaper journalist under the tutelage of Andy Harmon at the Hattiesburg, Mississippi *American*. Mr. Harmon taught me much more than the basics of gathering material for and writing news stories. For instance, one day when I had worked for him less than a month, he put his arm around my shoulders and said, "J. D., see those folks over there?" And he pointed at the advertising department downstairs.

"Yessir," I responded.

"Well, I don't ever want to see you associating with any of them on any level, socially or business-wise," Mr. Harmon continued, and I could tell by the look on his face and the tone of his voice that he was serious.

I didn't know what to say to that, so I shook my head and mumbled something like, "Uh huh."

"If you fraternize with them, they'll ruin you as a newsman," he concluded.

Andy Harmon was my first newspapering hero and mentor, and I never forgot that admonition. It has served me well.
I've seen more than one promising reporter go wrong because
of associating with advertising people. Some fell so far they
went into public relations. Every magazine and newspaper I
know about that has allowed the business side to dictate to its
editorial people, even a little, has lost the respect of the community, and in cases where there was significant competition, eventually ceased publication altogether or sold out to a
chain, or to the competition. As huge corporations slowly but
surely take control of the nation's media, there are fewer and
fewer independent, thinking newspapers, which in turn
causes the general public to have less and less respect for
newspapers and newspaper people.

Driving through the country, on or off the interstates, you'll
find that the majority of daily newspapers look almost exactly alike, front to back, and carry more or less the same
editorial pages and Op-Ed columns. That's not the way it's
supposed to be. When towns were still key factors in the national economy and politics, there were several small- and
medium-sized daily editors, working well away from the population centers, whose opinions were widely sought by big
national magazines, pundits, and political leaders. Among the
better known of these editors was Hodding Carter, of
Greenville, Mississippi, father of Hodding Carter, III, who now
writes a syndicated column out of Washington, D. C., is seen
occasionally on television news commentary panels, and was
at one time spokesperson for President Jimmy Carter's State
Department.

I was packing to move to Greenville to be managing editor of his newspaper in 1954, when the senior Hodding was
officially proclaimed a liar by a resolution by the Mississippi
House of Representatives, sponsored by one Eck Windham,

which referred specifically to an article by Carter that appeared in *Look*, and generally to just about everything else the Mississippi Delta journalist had written since moving to Greenville from Hammond, Louisiana, thirty years earlier.

Fifty years later, I forget exactly what the *Look* article was about, but I do remember that this was the year of the Supreme Court's public decision abolishing segregation in public schools. I was very young then, even for my age, and I had a few uncertain moments about what I might be getting myself into by going to work for Hodding Carter. There was little or no crusading fire in my belly at that time. But I had been scratching the itch of a growing suspicion that newspapering was too important to be practiced in the manner of the paper I worked for in Jackson. I didn't know a lot about Hodding Carter then, but what I did know made me think that he, too, regarded the newspaper profession as playing a more vital role in the community than that of just one more affluent member of the Chamber of Commerce.

So I agreed to a cut in pay and ignored the dire warnings of friends, who told me that Hodding Carter was hated and reviled by all right thinking citizens of the great State of Mississippi, and that I would wind up hanging beside him if I went. I moved to the Delta town, and it turned out to be quite a move.

Unlike some legends, the one that grew up around Hodding Carter was supported by realities. He really was fearless, as an editorial writer and as a man. He never forgot that he was, basically, a news reporter, and that a newspaper is only as good as its reporters. He knew how important a free press is to a community and a nation—one free not only of interference from the government but also free of interference from its advertisers. He did not believe a newspaper held its readers by being a mirror of community opinions and attitudes.

Hodding told me that a newspaper should be busily turning over rocks to see what was under them, then, once the community saw what turned up and started dealing with it, a newspaper should move on to other rocks. "A newspaper should be the conscience of the community," he told me many times. "It should never let the community rest on its laurels."

Hodding gave me and my staff genuine freedom to put out the daily editions as we saw fit. The only complaint he ever made about the way we ran the show was to say occasionally, "Hey, Jay, the paper's been kinda dull lately." That sort of remark always got us busy looking for new rocks to turn over.

At Hodding's *Delta Democrat-Times*, you sat at your typewriter with a sharp sense of purpose and place. There was a living challenge hovering over your shoulder—not a restricting challenge, but a challenge to dig deeper, write better, aim sharper than ever before. When I wrote an unsigned editorial, I knew many readers would assume Hodding had written it. Rather than inhibiting me, my awareness of the Hodding connection made me think tougher. Hodding catered to no sacred cows. I was convinced he would be disappointed in me, maybe even angry, if I did.

Through the "silent fifties" the *Delta Democrat-Times* yelled, pleaded, and preached about such gut issues as black voting rights and equal justice in the courts. Yet we did not lose one advertiser in all those years—surely a lesson for publishers today who steer clear of controversy for business reasons.

A few years after I moved on to New York City and the *Herald Tribune* in 1958, Ross Barnett was governor of Mississippi. One of those professional ex-communists who testified for a living, Barnett was called to Jackson where he earned his fee by implying, in that by-then-familiar oblique manner, that various past acquaintances and activities "proved"

Hodding was either a communist or a communist dupe. When this story appeared, a group of Greenville citizens, many of whom had fought Hodding on most local issues through the years, bought advertising space in the Jackson newspaper and declared, in so many words, that Hodding might be an SOB, but he damn sure wasn't a commie or commie dupe, and it was an insult to the people of Greenville to insinuate that he was.

Celebrities, dignitaries and notables from several worlds used to stop over in Greenville for some of the famous Carter hospitality if they came within a hundred or so miles. In the early fifties, a well-known black writer came through at a time when the Carter's guest accommodations were already occupied. After a few drinks, Hodding and Betty fashioned a turban for him with a fancy towel and escorted him downtown to the Greenville Hotel, where he was treated like a visiting sultan, which the hotel clerk no doubt assumed he was.

I remember how surprised I was when I first realized that Hodding was a serious name-dropper. He frequently sprinkled throughout his anecdotes and reminiscences the names of men and women who were nowhere near as widely known or highly esteemed as he was himself. One evening at the Carters' home only a few weeks after I moved to Greenville, a group gathered in the cypress grove between downtown Greenville and the Mississippi River Bridge. I was seated on the floor, leaning against Hodding's chair. All around the room, sprawled in various stages of repose, were genuine stars of Hollywood, Broadway and American literature. Elia Kazan was there. And Budd Schulberg, Robert Penn Warren, Eli Wallach and a couple of other luminaries whose names have escaped me over the years. I do recall that my contribution to the scintillating conversation flowing all around me that evening was slim to none. Gatherings such as this inspired me to try to catch up on my reading, (my masters degree from Mississippi Southern University notwithstanding).

Greenville was a bit more culturally evolved than your average small Southern town, and a great deal of its shine was due to the presence of the Carters for more than thirty-five years. There was also a bank president whose grandfather, William Alexander Percy, had written the classic book *Lanterns on the Levee*. And there was the patrician Ben Wasson, who had peddled his good friend William Faulkner's first novel. And Bern Keating, who was selling essays to *The New Yorker* and other national magazines. The woman's page editor at Hodding's newspaper, Louise Crump, had published a couple of novels, as well. Even the proprietor of Greenville's finest department store regularly played in a chamber music group and wrote Gothic fiction, although he stored it in a trunk and never submitted it for publication. Pretty stimulating company for a Lubbock boy.

Hodding had won, in 1946, a Pulitzer for editorials urging racial understanding—long before the Warren Supreme Court's school desegregation decision. He authored a dozen or so books, mostly dealing with Southern history and issues. His byline was known to readers of the *New York Times Sunday Magazine, Look, Saturday Evening Post* and other national publications. He was a Neiman Fellow at Harvard and permanent member of the Pulitzer selection committee. Several universities saw fit to bestow honorary degrees upon him, Harvard included. He sailed the Atlantic Ocean in a forty-two-foot schooner when he was in his fifties, swam the treacherous currents of the Mississippi River in his mid-forties on a five-dollar bet, and so on. Yet, he always described himself as "a damn good reporter who married Betty Werlein."

A few months before Hodding died in April of 1972 at the age of sixty-five, my young daughter Carter and I visited

Greenville. Hodding was suffering then from a recurrent dementia that caused him to lose his place now and then, especially when he was tired. Shortly after noon, we went by to see the Carters, and Betty led me upstairs where she had just put her husband to bed. He had been fine until just a few minutes prior to our arrival, she said, when his mind began wandering. After I had introduced Carter to Hodding, Betty took her downstairs and left Hodding and me alone. When they left, he motioned for me to come closer.

"I'm having them build this boat," he said, "and when it's finished we're going to pick four hundred people we like best and invite them to sail away with us to Japan or somewhere far away. I want you along."

I was so flattered to be included in Hodding's fantasy-trip that tears came to my eyes. Later, downstairs, Betty told me she had a persistent nightmare that somebody down on the Gulf Coast was actually building Hodding's boat.

"Hodding sounds so normal on the phone," she said with a sad smile, "that he might convince them he's serious."

How had such a man become the editor of the Greenville newspaper? As the story goes, William Alexander Percy, the poet-planter, and several other Greenville citizens got together in the early 1930s to look for someone who would give the town a lively, intelligent, progressive newspaper. They recruited the brash young editor-publisher of a tiny daily in Hammond, Louisiana, whose paper was going down for the third time because he refused to knuckle under to the pressures applied by the Huey Long regime. The Percy group put up the money for a new Greenville daily and let Hodding buy them out as soon as it succeeded financially. Details of that success story are now journalism history. The best version is Hodding's own book, *Where Main Street Meets the River.*

In 1980, the following was a *New York Times* wire service story lead:

SANTA ANA, CALIF.—*The Delta Democrat-Times*, a daily newspaper in Greenville, Mississippi, that has won a reputation over the last forty-two years as a courageous voice for civil rights in the Deep South, has been purchased by Freedom Newspapers, Inc., a California-based chain noted for espousing the most conservative editorial policies of any newspaper group in the country.

Stanley Walker, Baron Of Black Sheep's Retreat

There once was a bar on West 40th Street in New York called "Bleeck's—Formerly Artists and Writers Club." It had been a speakeasy during the prohibition years and when I was in New York from 1958 to 1961, it still retained that expensive, heavy wood look about it that most of us see only on reruns of *Cheers*. *Herald Tribune* newsroom hands gathered there to drink and talk after working hours as they waited to catch a train home for the night. I rarely stopped by that I didn't hear stories about Stanley Walker, the Texan who'd been city editor of the *Trib* during New York City journalism's juiciest era—the thirties and forties. Although he had been gone more than a decade by then, *Herald Tribune* old-timers talked as if Stanley had only been away a few weeks. They said he used to run his city room from Bleeck's much of the time, and showed me the table where he and his reporters carried on their match games. The winners got to kick the losers on the shin under the table. Tom O'Hara—rated a better reporter than his novelist brother John, who also had worked at the *Trib*—knew as many Stanley Walker stories as anybody. So did L. L.

Engelking, who hired me and who had been Stanley's city night editor in the golden years.

When I headed back home to Texas in 1961, Mr. Engelking wrote a letter of introduction ahead to Stanley. I hadn't been back long before I wrote him myself and, after receiving an invitation, drove down from Fort Worth to visit the legend.

Stanley's ranch was situated in Lampasas County, about halfway between Waco and Austin, on a back road. In his prompt reply to my first letter, Stanley gave me these directions to the small ranch he called "Black Sheep's Retreat":

> . . . the way to get here is to drive down Highway 281 through Hamilton, Evant, and then a poor little place called Adamsville. About eight miles south of Adamsville, almost at the top of a long rise in the road, you will see a mailbox labeled "Cox" on the lefthand side. Well, that ain't me, but turn in there anyhow and drive three miles on a dirt road. Rather suddenly you will perceive a beautiful valley, a veritable paradise. Straight ahead will be the old cabin, green with red-roofed outbuildings. And to the left, across a little stream, is another house, partly hidden back of some live oaks. This second house is the one to aim for. We live there most of the time. It is sometimes called "The Culture Club." The old green cabin is known as the "Pioneer Museum," and I live there part of the time. The hardier guests also like it.

He continued:

Be sure and let me know a day or two ahead of
time when you intend to arrive. Also, please
fetch me at least one bottle of bourbon, for which
I shall pay you. We are in dry territory, and I
use every device to run liquor in. . . . I'd advise
you to spend more than a few hours. You may
want to settle for a month, or a year, or forever.
On the other hand, I have known visitors who
couldn't get away fast enough. The joint is remarkably comfortable from my point of view,
but some persons find it a little primitive. You
can quickly size up the situation when you arrive. . . . We have some fruit flies. Also house
flies, horn flies, screwworm flies, bottle flies,
horse flies and so on. At the moment we seem
to have aphids in rather alarming numbers. We
have hummingbirds, great horned owls, rattle-
snakes and many other wonderful things.

I had written that I might drive on to Austin after visiting
him. "When you drive off to Austin," he wrote, "there is a
possibility that I may hitch a ride, for I'm due an Austin visit.
I do not drive a car—not that I can't but when I came here I
saw those signs: IF YOU DRIVE DON'T DRINK; IF YOU DRINK
DON'T DRIVE! Never did a man make an easier decision."

That was my first letter from him. It was signed: "Yours,
Stanley, Cattle Baron (Third Class), Patriot, Thinker, and Admirer of Grover Cleveland and Jack Johnson."

Until you adjust to its presence, a living legend can rattle
your nerves. You expect too much too soon, for one thing,
and probably fear you will stack up poorly. It was like that
when I met Stanley that first time, although his greeting at

the picket gate was ordinary enough. We sat awhile on the front porch of the Culture Club and watched the sun go down and the rain clouds roll in, as we both tossed out test lines. Stanley, who was dressed in a three-piece suit and tie, paced a lot and concentrated on swatting flies with an old-fashioned flap swatter. Soon, however, we got around to newspaper talk, so it was late when his wife Ruth made us call it a night. No matter where you find newspaper people, they will talk shop as long as their voices hold out.

Next morning, Stanley showed me around. He said his land consisted of only the worst corner of his father's ranch, and that his father had left it to him only because he feared Stanley would contest the will if he left him nothing. Stanley had paid the taxes on the place through the years. He was proud of what he and Ruth had done to and on the hardscrabble acreage. Juicy pasture grass waved all around, and two small, clear streams converged between the Culture Club and the Pioneer Museum. Sun-bleached stone fences stood white on the hillsides. The fences were about waist high and fifteen or twenty feet long. Stanley said he built the fences himself, selecting each stone carefully, so the wind and water wouldn't erode them. I asked what the fences were good for.

"Well," he said, "they help stop erosion some maybe, and the stock like to stand behind them in stormy weather. Mainly, they're beautiful."

The cattle were sleek and fat and exceptionally serene. So were the sheep. He sold stock only to those people he felt would appreciate the high quality of the meat, and the ranch had at last begun to show a profit, Stanley said. The Walkers appeared to live a somewhat Spartan life there, but they ate like discriminating millionaires. They grew most of their own vegetables and drank good wine with meals. It was a good life, greatly simplified and lacking little they regarded as important. Many Americans say they long for the simple life the Walkers achieved, but very few vigorously go after it. Stanley said he knew people who labored arduously to get away from the farm, then struggled for years trying to make enough to get back there, but never quite made it because they thought, mistakenly, that it took more funds than they ever would be able to accumulate. He and Ruth just up and did it.

A slightly built man with a hawk nose and a pipe forever in his teeth, Stanley always paced as he talked. It was never difficult to imagine him as he must have been in the *Herald Tribune* newsroom in the thirties and forties, helping some of journalism's finest reporters to reach their potential: Joseph Alsop, John Lardner, Joe Mitchell, Alva Johnson, L. L. Engelking, Tom Waring, Don Wharton, Joel Sayre, St. Clair McKelway, Lucius Beebe, Tom O'Hara (John O'Hara, Stanley said, had the ability but never got interested enough), Beverly Smith, James T. Flexner, and others. Gene Fowler had called Stanley "the last of the great New York city editors." Maggie Higgins, who came from Chicago to work for the *Herald Tribune* and won a Pulitzer covering the Korean War, devoted an entire chapter to Stanley in one of her books.

Stanley's stories about his newspaper days usually began with: "It was a hot Sunday afternoon in the newsroom." When he hired Lucius Beebe, for example, it was a hot Sunday afternoon. Stanley was at his desk, looking around at his coatless, sweating staff.

"I was thinking," he said, "what a grubby bunch they were, when this young man in immaculate formal morning attire walked up and spoke to me. He said his name was Lucius Beebe and he carried a fat scrapbook under one arm. He said he wanted a job. I told him he was hired. He said I hadn't even looked at his scrapbook. I said it didn't matter, he would add a little class to the joint." Beebe became famous for covering stories while dressed in evening clothes.

One of Stanley's legendary abilities was his talent for taking green reporters and turning them into stars. He almost had to fire a very green, young Joseph Alsop before he managed to teach him what he wanted from his reporters. "Then," Stanley said, "he became one of the best."

The process of turning good reporters into great reporters was sometimes filled with notable episodes that added grist to the Stanley Walker legend mill. For example, there was the time he tried to cure a reporter named Solomon of using too many semi-colons. "Solomon was a first-rate reporter," Stanley told me. "But he was obsessed with semi-colons. He insisted on using semi-colons indiscriminately. Finally, one hot Sunday afternoon in the newsroom, I decided to do something about it. I decided to file the semi-colon off his typewriter. And that's exactly what I did. Filed it right off. Then the sunuvabitch started putting 'em in with his copy pencil! What could I do?"

● ● ●

I stayed at Black Sheep's Retreat for three days that first visit. Stanley offered to deed me one of his grassy hills for ten dollars if I would agree to build a cabin on it within a year and live there at least part of each year. At the time, the offer was flattering, but not particularly appealing to me for various reasons—none of which seem sufficient now to explain why I didn't take him up on the deal. But I didn't.

"Our daily life here hasn't been easy," Stanley said as we wandered among his prize livestock the second morning of my visit, "but it is pleasant to feel you are making something out of nothing."

Ruth was every bit as absorbed by and devoted to newspaper lore and the journalism profession as Stanley. Unlike her husband, however, she was a child of the city, a music critic, an Eastern Intellectual. She and Stanley had been roommates for some time before leaving New York on a train on their way to Black Sheep's Retreat. "When we crossed the Red River," Stanley recalled, "I told Ruth, 'Honey, we're gonna have to get married in Dallas. This is Texas.'"

And they did. Dallas friends arranged the simple wedding, and they spent their honeymoon in the Adolphus Hotel. Then they were on their way to homestead Black Sheep's Retreat. They cleared the brush and most of the rocks off the wild ranch land themselves, hiring out only that work they could not possibly do by themselves. They built three dams and many terraces, erected some outbuildings, drilled a new well (with help), and planted fruit trees and a vegetable garden. The house they called the Pioneer Museum had been there when the newlyweds arrived in 1948. They bolstered the rotting walls, evicted the rats, snakes and squirrels, and lived in it while they built the Culture Club out of concrete blocks. Stanley did most of his writing in the Pioneer Museum, whose weathered exterior was unpainted, and the whole structure tilted slightly to the left.

Most of Stanley's two thousand or so books were shelved there. He had installed a new hardwood log mantle piece above the huge fireplace which provided the only heat in the drafty old house. Stanley sometimes slept in the Pioneer Museum when he was writing.

He denied that the ranch life was lonely after living in Manhattan for twenty-five years. "There is no loneliness here," he said. "Too much is happening, all of it interesting and some of it as fresh and new to me as a great newspaper just off the press. Loneliness must be a strange malady that afflicts only those who are inwardly impoverished."

Also, he claimed, living on the ranch greatly improved his health. "In a quarter of a century in New York, I had pleurisy at least a dozen times, pneumonia three times and was one of the great sniffers and snuffers of history."

Civilization, to Stanley, had to do with humanity, not appurtenances. "I have a well-to-do friend who fancies himself highly civilized," he said. "He has two bathtubs but no books in his New York apartment. I have no bathtubs and two thousand books. Which of us is civilized?"

Symbols did not interest the Baron of Black Sheep's Retreat. Humankind did. Neighbors said he was too sympathetic toward the outcasts of their community. As a member of the Lampasas Grand Jury one year, he filibustered until felony charges against three "poor whites" were reduced to misdemeanors. The country prosecutor complained, "we'd never indict anybody if Walker was on the Grand Jury every session." Ruth told me that story.

The "preoccupation with the masses" that was popular in some circles rankled Stanley. He saw it as another protective affectation of the insecure. "It is interesting," he said, "how most articulate underdog-lovers are usually well-heeled, and sound off in places that cost a lot of money just to sit down in. They seem to love the underdog en masse only, or as a general principle. But watch their noses wrinkle when they come face-to-face with real poverty."

Throughout the spring and summer of 1962, I visited Stanley several times. I was traveling a great many miles, getting reacquainted with my home state after an absence of almost fifteen years. Some friends and I purchased a 1949 black Cadillac hearse from a friendly used hearse dealer in Dallas, for $75, put in a new battery, and converted the business end into a mobile sleeping quarters. I traveled mostly out of Austin, writing for *The Texas Observer* and, until it finally folded after a lengthy strike, the *Herald Tribune*'s Op-Ed pages. Willie Morris, perhaps the state's highest profile liberal back then, was editor of *The Observer*, and another friend, Jim Leonard, was serving a season as executive director of the state Republican Party. I thought it would be interesting to take Republican Jim Leonard and Liberal Willie Morris to Black Sheep's Retreat for an evening with world class iconbuster, Stanley Walker, so I wrote to Stanley. He answered:

> Dear Col. Milner:
>
> By all means come up some Saturday or Sunday, bringing a bottle and of course the puissant Willie Morris. If indeed there is such a person, you may also bring Ronnie Dugger, but if there really is, I'd like to examine him. Better notify me before you come so I can thaw out some meat, put in my teeth, etc.
>
> I hear little from the strange new *Herald Tribune*. I still do book reviews for them, but the special articles seem to be out. The paper is not a newspaper but a sort of daily magazine. Maybe they are on the right track, but damned if I get it. You can fool around with typographical boondoggling all you please, but (from my point of view) a good story is still a good story. Remember what the great Mr. Dana said in answering some idiot's question about the nature of the newspaper business— "It's buying paper, putting some words on it, and selling it for a profit."
>
> I am eager to see your hearse. May I shoot a Ku Kluxer and give it a workout?

Carry on, jabbing with the left and then duck-
ing.

Yours for G. Cleveland & Sound Money
S. Walker, Consulting Editor, "The Lay
Brother," official organ of the Central
Texas Association Opposed to
Artificial Insemination.
P.S.—Better make the trip fairly soon. I think I
am entering my THIRD childhood and there are
weevils in my cortex.

We had a fine time that trip, although Willie Morris hadn't
been able to make it, and Stanley seemed distracted. About a
month later, I was surprised to receive another letter, asking
me if I would drive my hearse into Lampasas and park it in
front of the county courthouse. Stanley said he would meet
me in town this time. It seems a local undertaker was cam-
paigning for some county office, and Mrs. Walker thought the
hearse parked at the courthouse would give them a few chuckles. "And we've needed a few chuckles around here of late,"
he added. Besides that, Stanley wrote, he would like to take a
ride in my hearse, since he had never ridden in one.

I arrived about the middle of a Saturday afternoon. Stanley
and I sipped hot coffee in a downtown cafe, waiting until Ruth
closed the library, which was in the courthouse. Then she
drove out to the ranch—about ten miles north of town, and
we were to follow immediately in the hearse. But the hearse
wouldn't start. After trying the starter so many times the bat-
tery began to sound weak, Stanley and I got out, lifted the
hood, stared at the engine awhile, fiddled with some wires,
kicked the tires, tried the starter again to no avail, and stared
at the engine some more. Then he telephoned for help. It
was almost dark when the young man arrived in an ancient

green pickup truck. He stared, tight-lipped, under the hood awhile, as we had done before him, then announced that he'd have to give us a pull. He said the hearse had "fluid drive," so he'd have to pull it pretty fast to start it. It was too heavy to push, he said.

The dilapidated old truck was leading us rapidly through the Lampasas business district when Stanley noted that our caravan appeared to be attracting an uncommon amount of attention among Saturday evening strollers along the main street. As we rattled by, they were doing double takes that would have done old-time silent movie directors proud.

"You'd think they've never seen a hearse being pulled by a green pickup truck before," Stanley remarked, a twinkle in his eyes.

It was about this time that we first noticed smoke curling up through cracks in the floorboard at our feet. We were whipping along and now folks were shouting at us, although we couldn't understand what they were saying. Stanley opened the door and leaned out. "We're on fire!" he announced solemnly as he slammed the door and lay back against the seat, his eyes closed.

I looked out my side. Sure enough, smoke was blowing up from beneath the hearse as we picked up speed and reached the outskirts of town. Then, the umbilical chain connecting us to the pickup snapped. I tried the horn, but it wasn't working. We both leaned out and bellowed at the young man in the pickup. We were a mile or so past the city limits, and I was stomping on the brakes when he saw the smoke and stopped.

As it turned out, there was more smoke than fire, and we were able to extinguish what little there was with some water we found in a ditch near the road. Then, wonder of wonders, the hearse started easily. We paid the young man and rested there awhile, catching our breath and letting our hearts slow down. Then I drove us, slowly and thoughtfully, back to Black Sheep's Retreat, leaving the young man standing beside his ancient truck scratching his head.

We had gone maybe a mile or two when Stanley started laughing. He said he supposed that was the most excitement they'd had in Lampasas in many a Saturday night. "Must have been some sight," he grinned, "seeing a flaming hearse being pulled down Main Street. Folks'll speculate on that for some time, I expect."

We had turned off the highway, and the lights of the Culture Club were visible through the trees at the foot of the hill, when Stanley said, "That's an experience that would cause any man to ponder—having his hearse catch on fire. It's almost as if the devil were rushing things there a bit."

I never saw him again after that visit. In November he took his own life with a shotgun. The "weevils in his cortex" had turned out to be cancer of the larynx. He had told Ruth he didn't believe he wanted to go along with God's little joke this time; she'd thought he was kidding, of course. He was sixty-three.

MAdDoG
DaYs

Good Ole
Billie Lee

In 1962, after bunking on the sofa at the South Austin home of Fletcher Boone—a struggling painter and sculptor who later co-owned the popular restaurant/bar "Raw Deal"—and his wife Jean, a local television personality who described her job as "showing Hill Country women how to get in and out of cars without showing their crotches," I moved into the hills in a concrete block cabin belonging to the parents of Joan Holloway. The Boones and Holloways were friends of my new sportswriter friend, Bud Shrake, who was also a friend and colleague of Joan Holloway's former husband, Dan Jenkins. Shrake had called ahead and asked the Boones to help me get settled in Austin. Jean Boone, Joan Holloway and Shrake, along with Dan Jenkins and his wife June, were all graduates of Paschal High School in Fort Worth, where my brother Wilbur Ray had gone and starred on the football team. In the first few months after I returned to Texas from New York I had begun to suspect that everybody had gone to Paschal but me. This was true of at least the majority of the instigators of the most mischief and fun we managed to get into. I sometimes felt as if I had walked into something that had been going on for a long time before I got there and was picking up speed along the way. The Maddog movement had been underway for a while and seemed to know where it was going. We actually had membership cards printed up with our Maddog slogan and logo (a line drawing of a crazed individual saying "Everything that isn't a mystery is guesswork.")

The Privileged Few founding fathers of Maddog, Inc. later grew beyond the confines of Austin and went international, with card-carrying members in far-flung places with strange sounding names—like England, France, and California. Some of the more celebrated later members of Maddog, Inc. who joined up with this motley yet remarkable band of servants to mankind over the years include Dennis Hopper, Willie Nelson, Peter Gent, and later, Woodrow Wilson Bean.

In the summer of 1962, Willie Morris asked if I would do him a favor and fill in as his associate editor at *The Texas Observer* until a young man who would be his permanent associate completed a Fulbright year in Europe in a couple of months. I had been living and working outside Texas for almost fifteen years and was all but totally ignorant on the ins and outs of current Texas politics, but I quit a good job at the State Democratic Executive Committee and joined Willie in the exhausting battle against the Philistines. I had replaced Billie Lee at the committee job, on his recommendation, and I was pleased to find myself on the fringe of a unique good old boy network, in more ways than one.

We were basically a merry band of newspaper crusaders and Good Time Charleys. It wasn't so much that we were trying to live Billie Lee's novel as it was that the book had drawn an uncannily accurate picture—if not of the way we were, then of the way we very often perceived ourselves. We

lived and worked in a more or less constant state of exulta-
tion and angst, a word I read for the first time in *The Gay
Place*. And when we greeted each other, we said, "Haw yew,"
just like Billie Lee's characters did. We exaggerated the
cadence and flatness of our Texas accents and articulations,
especially when in the company of those we somewhat snidely
regarded as being on the pompous side.

We listened with fervor to good country music—long before country was cool. And we listened to jazz, particularly
the cool jazz of Dick Harp, both before and after Kiz died.
(Remember the 90th Floor in Dallas?) In Austin, we went to
Mr. Kenneth Threadgill's place on weeknights so we wouldn't
have to contend with the weekend throngs of music lovers
(whom we later learned embodied the likes of Janis Joplin),
and Mr. Threadgill could be nearly always be persuaded to
sing along with his Jimmy Rodgers jukebox records. Sometimes Shorty picked for him.

We created our own myths and legendary characters of
ourselves and each other and happily spread these legends
by word of mouth and through bits and pieces of our writings
for various newspapers and magazines. The legend of Billie
Lee Brammer was the most enduring—for a number of reasons, both estimable and odious. Brammer's legend was not
spun out of whole cloth. We had a lot of help from Billie Lee
himself, although not by his design.

Not long after I met Billie Lee Brammer in the winter of
1962, we went to a party at Willie Morris's house in west Austin. At the close of each legislative session, Willie would an-
nounce the winners of his annual Neanderthal Awards and
throw a party in their honor. The guests were current winners and their adversaries on Capitol Hill, which made for a
lively time. I remember one Neanderthal following Willie

around most of that night trying to convince him he was no dumbbell.

"Shoot fire, Willie," he said repeatedly, "I've read *Prowst* and all them."

That was the night Brammer's ex-wife Nadine summoned him from the party to babysit with their children while she went out. Billie Lee asked if I would mind taking his date Janie home if he didn't make it back to Willie's party. As it turned out, he never made it back. Janie, a pretty UT undergraduate he'd been seeing regularly, was still in a party mood when the last of Willie's guests headed home, so we repaired to my apartment to listen to a new album I'd bought that day. She fell asleep on my couch as the music played and I was unable to rouse her, so I went to bed and left her there snoring daintily.

Early next morning, my phone jangled me awake. It was Linda, Brammer's date's roommate. She said she'd called to warn us that Billie Lee was terribly upset because Janie had spent the night with me.

"He sat in this car outside your window all night in the cold," she said, "staring up at your light and imagining lurid scenarios."

I called him and we met at Scholz's, considered by serious problem-solvers and critics-at-large in those days to be Austin's most beloved beer garden. The misunderstanding was soon dispelled. Billie Lee was much too placid to successfully hold a grudge.

He and I had first met at the old New Orleans Club. Fletcher Boone introduced us. Billie Lee had only recently moved back to Texas from Atlanta where he worked for *Time* magazine. *The Gay Place* had hit town less than a year earlier and Austin was still reverberating from the impact. Almost everyone seemed to be trying to prove, by the way they lived and talked, that Brammer had based at least one of the novel's characters on them. I had read *The Gay Place* in New York a few months earlier and remember feeling a tiny resentment toward Brammer before I met him. I had a sneaky hunch that his novel was better than mine, which had come out a month or so before we met.

Anyway, Billie Lee and I became friends, and I found myself running with the crowd that more or less orbited around him. Austin always seemed to embrace a star of the moment, someone everyone sought to wind up at the same party with. Willie Morris was also hot in Austin then, but Willie and Billie Lee were usually at the same parties, so that simplified matters. (A decade later, Austin's proclivity to lionize stars-of-the-moment would go out of control as Austinites went more or less crazy over another Willie—along with Jerry Jeff and other picker poets. These guys not only wrote well, but they sang what they wrote under spotlights, which attracted even larger and more vigorous entourages.) In the early and mid-sixties, it was Billie Lee and Willie Morris everybody wanted to hang out with. At least everyone of a certain liberal and perhaps intellectual turn of mind. It was a crowd once in a while referred to, not always lovingly, as "the *Observer* crowd."

The *Observer* was a weekly tabloid then. On Thursdays, when it came out, the floor of both houses of the state legislature resembled one of those old *Philadelphia Inquirer* ads. (You may remember them. There'd be a crowd of people on a commuter train or in a restaurant and all but one would be reading the *Inquirer* and the caption would read: "Almost everyone reads the *Inquirer*.") Before he went to work for Lyndon Johnson in Washington in the late 1950s, Brammer had been an *Observer* associate editor under founder Ronnie Dugger's editorship.

I soon discovered that Brammer wrote at night, or tried to. He told me he wrote *The Gay Place* while working for *Time* on the White House night shift. Since very little news breaks at the White House at night, he was free to work on his novel. To stay awake he swallowed diet pills. That's the story he told me. I've heard others over the years.

Billie Lee said he wrote what became part three of *The Gay Place* first and sent it to Houghton Mifflin. They liked it, but felt it was too short and asked him to add to it. He then wrote what became part two. When his editor read that, he apparently became excited about what he had and asked Billie Lee to add still more. Brammer then wrote part one, which many consider the best of the three parts.

One morning after somebody's party, Billie Lee and I were watching the sunrise from a hillside overlooking Lake Travis, and he confided that he was afraid he couldn't write a real novel—that he didn't know how. He said that sometimes late at night, when he was alone at his typewriter and the pills were kicking in, he believed he could do it again, but in the cold light of day he was afraid he didn't know how.

Billie Lee was sensitive about being short. I don't know how tall he was, but I don't believe I would have noticed his stature at all if he hadn't talked about it so much. I was six-two and he made reference to my height many times. "If I was as tall as you are," he'd say wistfully, "I'd have it made." I'd say, "Then how come I don't?" and he would grin and change the subject. I once asked him why he quit working for LBJ. He muttered that the Senator insisted on calling him "Boy."

He had been an athlete in high school, I think, but I never saw him exercise on purpose in all the years I knew him. And

I seldom saw him sleep. He always seemed to be getting ready to do something or was just finishing something. I've dropped by his abode as late as 3:00 A.M., and found him brewing up a pot of chili. I never actually saw him reading, but he had always read that new book I was planning to read and had always heard every new album the good word was out on. I assumed he did all his reading and music listening while the rest of us slept.

A time or two, Billie Lee and I tried to rent a house together. He had a great talent for finding the best, most unusual, out-of-the-way houses and apartments. He would find one and move in, but before I could get loose from my lease, he would get evicted for one reason or the other—often for too many parties or, in one instance, his odd hours. He once found this marvelous house on the lake just outside Austin. It was a guest house, actually, located in a stand of trees behind the main house where a retired couple lived. One day the woman from the main house stopped me and asked what it was Mr. Brammer did for a living. I told her he was a writer.

"His lights are on all night," she said nervously. "People come and go all night long. It's driving me crazy." She gave us the rent money we'd paid her and asked Billie Lee to move out. He had been there less than a month. I hadn't even moved in yet.

One night I stopped by Billie Lee's apartment near the University campus with Malcolm McGregor, an El Paso attorney who was in the state House of Representatives back then. Billie Lee was sitting at his electric Smith-Corona, typing away, so we stayed only a few minutes. As we were leaving, a gang of revelers from Scholz's invaded the place. McGregor offered to kick everybody out so he could work, but Billie Lee asked him not to, saying they were friends and probably would leave pretty soon anyway. We left, making sure everyone could hear us tell Billie we were going because, "We know you have to work." I forget now where we went from there, but shortly after midnight we drove back by Billie Lee's place just to check. Sure enough, the party was still going strong. We went in and found Billie Lee sitting alone in a corner, on the floor, sipping a Dr. Pepper longneck. The clamorous party caroused round him, none of the exhilarated guests paying any attention to their amiable, but silent, host.

I sat down beside him on the floor. He nodded, grinning his characteristically sheepish grin, and asked solemnly, "Am I this much fun?"

Billie Lee had a rare charisma. Strange and powerful. His compelling charm had something to do with the fact that he had written that famous book everyone had read, or heard about, and perhaps related to. But it was more than that. One friend, Jim Smithum, might have come pretty close to explaining his mysterious charm when he said, "Billie Lee is the most reasonable human being I ever knew." It could be that the crowd so often ended up at Billie Lee's simply because the lights were always on, but I think not. That, no doubt, was part of it, but not all. I never heard Billie Lee raise his voice, and he was one of the best listeners I ever encountered. He always appeared to be deeply interested in what you were saying and knew something about whatever subject you were talking about.

As his body became increasingly tolerant to the contents of the ever-present diet pills, Billie Lee's need for more and more grew and grew. Innumerable women felt protective of this quiet little man who had written the book that had moved them so and to demonstrate their dedication, they would volunteer to scavenge pills for him. Billie Lee's favorite scam was that he had arranged "this great deal" for the temporary use of a friend's cabin in the hills and wanted to gather in a month's supply to go off by himself up there and finish his book. I have been with him when as many as five women came by his apartment in one afternoon to bestow upon him a stash of cabin-in-the-hills, finish-the-book medication.

He would stash his "heart medicine," as he called the diet pills, in tricky hiding places so his friends couldn't find them and obtain the use of a few from him when he wasn't home. He never bothered to lock his doors and people wandered in and out twenty-four hours a day. One day I stopped by and, while awaiting his arrival, turned on the radio. When he walked in and heard the music, he moaned and quickly snatched up a baggie from the guts of the radio. The tubes had heated up and melted the pills hidden there into a sticky green glob. He deposited the baggie in the refrigerator to solidify, then ate the hardened glob like a cookie.

Houghton Mifflin looked forward to Billie Lee's second book and paid him several advances for it. His agent was also anxious to see it completed, and for years a number of major East Coast critics kept an eye out for its release. Gore Vidal had called *The Gay Place,* winner of the prestigious Houghton Mifflin fiction prize and several other awards, an "American classic."

Billie Lee's second novel was to be a sequel to *The Gay Place.* The working title was "Fustian Days" and, at one time in 1962, he had written more than a hundred pages. I read them and in my opinion they were vintage Brammer, at his fluid best. There were about a hundred and fifteen pages, best I remember. Roy Sherwood, Billie Lee's protagonist in part one of *The Gay Place,* was the main character. Roy has been elected to congress from Texas and is in Washington getting his vibes going in the right direction to be a congressman. He has an empathy for the lot of women which is ahead of his time. He lives an altruistic existence, although occasionally

somewhat reluctantly, and his lifestyle is relatively free of
the constraints imposed upon him by the Southern mentality
of his family, but he fights his existential inclinations as hard
as he fights those inherited from his fundamentalist parents.
He always shows up for the party, but looks as if he'd rather
be someplace else—maybe in a cabin in the hills, with his
dog, or in a tent on Padre Island with a wench. It is obvious
that the hero of "Fustian Days" had a great deal in common
with his creator.

Sherwood is the character Paul Newman said he wanted
to play when they did the movie from *The Gay Place*. The
film group formed around Newman's stardom included
Oscar-winning director Martin Ritt and others involved in making the movie *Hud* from McMurty's first novel, *Horseman Pass
By*—a film that had boosted Newman's film stardom considerably. They paid Billie Lee for the screen rights to his book
and Ritt, Newman, and others came to Austin to search for
locations for filming. The deal fell through after Billie Lee's
ex-wife, Nadine, filed a suit claiming she was due a share of
any monies of any kind or character that might change hands
in the name of *The Gay Place*, since it was written while she
and Billie Lee were man and wife in the eyes of the law as
well as the Lord. Last I heard, James Garner had purchased
film rights to *The Gay Place* from the Paul Newman/Martin
Ritt group, but that was a long time ago.

Anyway, in those opening scenes of Billie Lee's "Fustian
Days" I read in 1962, Roy Sherwood had just arrived in Washington, D. C., to serve his first term in Congress and was wandering around the District, absorbing and reliving the history
represented by the stony likenesses of the memorials and
the monuments in honor of the country's heroes, while day-
dreaming about all he might accomplish there, politically and
sexually, as an heir to those personages who made this coun-

try what it is and isn't today. There was, in those few pages, an atmosphere of joyful angst, similar to that of the opening pages of *The Gay Place.*.

Not long after I read those provocative pages, Billie Lee received from Gloria Steinem a job offer he couldn't refuse. He was given a thousand-dollar advance on the salary he would receive for spending two weeks in Helsinki helping put out a newspaper at an international youth festival to be held there. It seems Russian students had published a much-admired newspaper at a previous festival, and our guys, green with envy, were determined to counter-publish at the next gathering. The deal, as Billie Lee explained it to me, was financed by our State Department, or some branch thereof (someone later said the CIA), and was to appear to be a spontaneous endeavor—conceived and carried out entirely by patriotic American youth. Evidently, the term "youth" was interpreted rather loosely, since Billie Lee was in his thirties, as were others he knew who would be involved in the project—all spontaneously endeavoring for our side.

Billie Lee badly needed the money (a candidate for Attorney General he had been writing speeches for having lost in the election), so he grabbed the job offer and the salary advance and booked passage on a freighter leaving Mobile, Alabama, on such-and-such date. The day he told me about the trip, he was so pleased he actually laughed out loud. Billie Lee grinned a lot, but seldom laughed. He said he planned to take along his trusty Smith-Corona portable electric, and go on an uninterrupted writing binge for the length of the voyage. When he disembarked at Le Havre, he would proceed to Helsinki, join his colleagues in putting out a dandy newspaper that would put the commies to shame, draw his remaining salary and catch another slow freighter back to the good old U.S. of A. and finish "Fustian Days" by the time he got home. This, he pointed out, would cause great joy in several camps, including his agent's, his ex-wife's, and his parents'— not to mention his own. He was laying in an adequate supply of heart medicine (everyone cooperated wonderfully on that project), and was ready, willing, and now able to get off his butt and out of his partying rut and back to some serious work and finish that derned novel if it killed him.

A few months later, I returned to Austin from wherever it was I'd been and was told that two things had gone wrong with Billie Lee's splendidly well-laid plan: First, there were no electrical outlets, as we Americans know them, on the foreign freighter, so he was unable to plug in his trusty Smith-Corona portable electric and write his heart out. And, since he had learned to do all of his creative thinking while seated at a typewriter, he had gotten no writing done at all. Second, due to several unscheduled detours to pick up cargo, the boat was three weeks late getting there and Billie Lee missed the entire festival.

He had spent the thousand-dollar advance so he arrived broke, a stranger in a strange land, with no job to go to and his supply of heart medicine seriously depleted. Although details are fuzzy to me still, somehow he made his way to Spain where an old girl friend was vacationing. She loaned him the money to get home. Women always took care of Billie Lee long after he quit taking care of them.

● ● ●

It wasn't a bunch of spaced out druggies doing all this partying around Billie Lee in those days. These were young, ambitious, sometimes hardworking journalists, trial lawyers and politicians who mixed and mingled with the college crowd. They were intellectually bent and liberally inclined, with a professional underdog here and there, and maybe one or two basic conservatives, tagging along for the good times.

His eccentricities grew, both in quantity and in depth of strangeness. He was far ahead of anyone else I knew or heard tell of in doing what was happening in the sixties. Not the protests and demonstrations, but the experimentation with hallucinogens. Billie Lee was a flower child who never let his hair grown long or costumed himself for the part. He went to San Francisco and did all the quintessential San Francisco things, along with Janis, Doug Sahm and certain other Texas musicians.

Increasingly, Billie Lee's days and nights began to pulsate around the pills. All day and all night, every day and every night. Planning to get more, getting more and planning to get more and so on and on, ad infinitum. It's not that the pills were all that difficult to come by in those days. There were physicians whose entire practices were devoted to prescribing diet drugs for upwardly mobile men and women who filled the doctors' waiting rooms with nervous chatter, wringing their hands as they waited in turn to see their own Dr. Feelgood. ("Oh, doctor, I'm having trouble sleeping now—could you give me something for that too?")

Even though he was more and more distant, Billie Lee still showed up, at least briefly, for most soirees and other Maddog social gatherings. This was characteristic of his increasingly idiosyncratic behavior, because before the pills became the essence of his existence, this shy, unobtrusive man had always preferred being with small groups of friends rather than big crowds. Billie Lee's demeanor remained quiet and reserved. He was never verbose the way most diet pill addicts were. He listened and watched, somewhat tenaciously. People were always saying, "Look at Billie Lee over there

watching us." I think most assumed he was gathering material. But looking back, I think he was living inside his head.

People still hung out at Billie Lee's. Among the most irresistible drawing cards there were his component hi-fi system
(state of the art for its time) and his colossal album collection. After the party dispersed and the rest of the civilized
world was asleep, while he relished his last bowl of chili, Billie
Lee must have laid back and listened to the latest albums.
Later, he would be forced to hock his hi-fi system to various
cronies whenever serious cash flow problems developed, as
they did more and more frequently as time went on. Last I
heard, the hi-fi was in Pete Gent's custody.

One afternoon, Billie Lee called and asked me to come to
his apartment. He had something he wanted me to hear. It
was the first Bobby Dylan album, the one with "Talking New
York Blues" on it. I had forgotten the name of the kid I'd failed
to interview in New York. Dylan sang with only his guitar
and harmonica as accompaniment. I remember thinking the
harsh, talking-singing style had to belong to an old-timer who
knew all the familiar routines as well as some fresh tricks.
Imagine my surprise when Billie Lee told me Dylan was only,
what? Twenty? Twenty-one? It was the damnedest bringing
up to date of country blues I'd ever heard, even if I wasn't
always completely sure what Dylan was singing. What the
heck does "jumping parking meters" mean? That is just the
kind of thing Billie Lee was always doing—guiding a friend
through a fascinating new experience.

● ● ●

In the fall of 1963, I was at Texas Tech, in my old home
town of Lubbock, as part-time advisor to the student staff of
the campus newspaper, which was going from weekly to daily

publication that year. This little chore would, I surmised, give me a chance to renew old palships of my youth; pick up where we'd left off all those many moons ago when we were young. (This didn't work out as I'd hoped it would, of course, but that's another story.) Near the end of the semester, I invited Billie Lee to come out and meet with those students who had expressed an interest in meeting the famous novelist. Arrangements were made for Billie Lee to give a speech at a luncheon meeting of the local professional journalism society to help defray expenses.

That evening with the Tech students, Billie Lee was at his most charming and eloquent best—sometimes even wise—just as he had been at the SDX meeting of professional journalists earlier. He told those West Texas kids stories that seemed to prove to them there really was a chance for them in the big leagues of journalism. That there really was a New York City where kids from places like Dalhart, Amarillo, Lubbock, Lamesa and other small towns could make it—if they wanted it badly enough, and knew what they were doing, and could spell. They'd all read *The Gay Place,* or professed to have read it, and many harbored secret aspirations of one day writing their own Great American Novel, as did almost every journalist I ever knew who was worth his salt. Billie Lee told them of covering the White House for *Time* and about how the horny young president of the United States had frequently satiated those passionate urges. I hadn't been in the company of Washington correspondents in awhile and wasn't up on the latest Capitol Hill watering hole gossip. I'd heard such rumors before leaving New York, but I generally attributed them to the fact that the new president was young and handsome. Also, by then I had learned that Billie Lee didn't always adhere stringently to the truth. He sometimes preferred to embellish it with the use of his ingeniously talented imagination and vast repository of frustrations. Plus, of course, Billie Lee got a kick out of telling a good story to an appreciative audience.

Not long after that visit to Lubbock, our young president was shot dead in Dallas. Lyndon Baines Johnson moved into the White House. Arthur Goddam Fenstemaker lived! A new paperback edition of the *The Gay Place* hit the racks of bookstores and supermarkets from coast to coast. On the jackets of the brand new paperback editions were quotes from Murray Kempton and Gore Vidal linking the fictional Fenstemaker to the living LBJ, head honcho of what was arguably the world's most powerful machinery. Kempton flat out called Billie Lee's Fenstemaker the best depiction of the president from Texas he'd ever read anywhere.

Many who insisted that Fenstemaker was Lyndon Johnson saw it as an anti-LBJ characterization—including, apparently, Johnson himself and members of his family. In point of fact, as Vidal indicated, Billie Lee wrote Fenstemaker as the leader of the good guys and a sympathetic character. But he is a raunchy son of a gun, with weaknesses of the flesh, which fact, ironically, probably accounts for the Johnson family's objections. As far as I know, the only public comment Johnson himself ever made about *The Gay Place* was in answer to a direct question— "What did you think of it?"—or words to that effect. Johnson was quoted as saying, "I don't read dirty books,"—or words to that effect. The ultimate irony is that Brammer told me he actually based the Fenstemaker character on the late Louisiana governor Earl Long, as much as on LBJ.

When Johnson took over the White House, it seemed quite natural for publishers to envision a bestselling nonfiction book about LBJ written by none other than the creator of Fenstemaker. A preliminary deal was struck and Billie Lee was soon on his way to Washington, D. C., where he planned to call on his friend Lyndon B. Johnson and ask for his cooperation, if not his blessing. To Billie Lee's surprise and not inconsiderable chagrin, Mr. President did not condescend to extend the hospitality of the oval office to the writer from Texas.

Billie Lee's surprise and chagrin stemmed from the fact that he regarded his friendship with Johnson as special. He had worked for Johnson when LBJ waged intra-mural war against John Kennedy for the party nomination. When Kennedy named Johnson as his running mate, Billie Lee (according to Al Reinert's introductory essay on Billie Lee in a Texas Monthly Press reissue of *The Gay Place*) put off proofing the galleys of his book to join the campaign trail on behalf of LBJ. As Reinert notes, Brammer "worked on Democratic press relations and white papers, drafted speeches for both candidates, traveled with Johnson on the cornpone special that held the South together for the Catholic presidential nominee. Not until after the election did Billie Lee go back to being a writer."

(Note, incidentally, that Billie Lee is spelled "Billy Lee" in the Texas Monthly edition, as it is in a number of other publications. However, I have a long handwritten letter from him—which I will publish in its entirety herein later—signed "Billie Lee.")

Billie Lee did nothing more about the proposed LBJ book, a fact which undoubtedly cost him a great deal of sorely-needed money, because publishers were offering rather generous advances.

By 1964, Willie Morris had moved from "north towards home" to Manhattan and into another one of its Golden Eras. Bud Shrake and Dan Jenkins had also moved to New York City about that time to write for *Sports Illustrated* and become

two of the leading contributors to that magazine's most interesting period, when it was noted for the quality of its writing.
Gary Cartright was in Philadelphia writing a column for one
of the big papers there. Larry L. King, in Washington, D. C.,
had thrown caution to the winds and quit his day job as administrative aide to a congressman to work full time at writing to find out for sure whether or not he could make it. One
of the first major articles, if not the first, King sold, was to Willie
Morris at *Harper's*. It was a piece on Washington's "Second Ba-
nanas," the administrative aides to congressmen. This launched
a new career for the thick-chested lad from West Texas. He
quickly became one of the handful of freelancers in America
making a living at it.

I heard along about that time that Billie Lee had spent
time in Washington with King, who was batching it in a tiny
room at the Dodge House, a residential hotel on Capitol Hill.
There was some talk, too, that Billie Lee had visited awhile
with Shrake and Jenkins in New York, where he'd received a
sizable advance from a sports magazine for an article he never
wrote. Somebody said Billie Lee went to California where he
happily wasted a period of time hanging out with Ken Kesey.
Word was that he was getting deeper and deeper into drug
experimentation. Or could what Billie Lee was doing still be
categorized with any validity as experimenting?

Billie Lee's adventures in chemistry weren't happening in
a vacuum. He wasn't out there all by himself experimenting
with LSD and other mind-expanding chemicals and herbs.
He was in the avant garde, you might say, of a rapidly flourishing drug culture in America. Over the next few years, I
would see Billie Lee only occasionally, usually when we were
in Austin at the same time. He never talked about finishing
"Fustian Days" anymore. At least not to me.

● ● ●

Meantime, change was blowing in the wind. I was in an office in the capital building in Austin one day when hundreds of uniformed Texas A&M students, all male, demonstrated against a proposal to admit females to Aggieland. I remember thinking this was, well, *odd* to say the least, this determination to ban all females from the manly population of College Station. Someone remarked that the reason I considered this behavior peculiar was that I just didn't understand the Aggie mindset. Which I'm sure was true.

On other Texas college campuses the issues weren't in such opposition to the times. Jerry Levias and James Cash—at SMU and TCU, respectively—ran Jim Crowism off the athletic fields of the Southwest Conference. Women everywhere were beginning to complain about their plight as second-class citizens. LBJ finally pushed through the civil rights bill that President Kennedy had been unable to get through the machinery of congress. The anti-Vietnam War movement was gaining strength across the country. Pretty people and pretty clothes were being abandoned in favor of the "natural" look. In educational institutions, everyone—even in Texas—was beginning to see fraternities and sororities as superfluous, at best.

Along about that time, Billie Lee met a young woman named Dorothy Brown, and in due time they decided to get married. Dorothy was a UT undergraduate from Houston. Her father was, as I understood it, a fairly typical Texas businessman, in that he wanted nothing but the best for his little girl, and the word was that he wasn't entirely thrilled with the match. Billie Lee was a decade or so older than Dorothy and, although various people claimed he had written a book of some kind, there were rumors that it was a dirty book and, anyhow, Billie Lee sure didn't look very prosperous and didn't even have a regular job.

Knowing there was some anxiety involved on the part of Billie Lee's prospective in-laws, his friends all solemnly vowed to be on their best behavior at the wedding and all the attendant nuptial festivities. The best man, a UT professor recently migrated from England to Texas, decided it would make a most admirable impression upon the family and friends of the bride for him to escort as his date to the wedding festivities a brilliant young lady lawyer and member of the state House of Representatives who was attracting attention around Austin those days because of her brains and eloquence. Her name was Barbara Jordan.

I missed the wedding and can't report with certainty, but I can just imagine Dorothy's father's reaction when he came to the realization he was throwing what was doubtless the first integrated wedding on his block.

In the summer of 1969 I was on my way back home to Fort Worth (where I'd been teaching journalism), after vacationing in Mexico City. I had driven all the way down and back, taking the scenic route home, and was road weary by the time I reached Austin. Bud Shrake had persuaded the managing editor of *Sports Illustrated* to let him work out of Austin instead of New York City, and he and his new wife, Doatsy, had moved into a nice split level in Westlake Hills. (Shrake's contention was that, since he was on the road all the time anyway, he might as well reside where he wanted to.) When I arrived in Austin I called Shrake and, as I had hoped, he invited me to spend the night at his house. It didn't take much to incite a celebration on any given night and somehow or another a party materialized that evening and Billie Lee appeared.

That particular night he showed up alone. Seems that Dorothy had left him. Run off to Mexico with a former member of the state legislature who had seen the light and joined the revolution for peace and good will—let his hair grow long and quit shaving his face. Billie Lee himself didn't volunteer all of this information. He never was one to bore you with his personal misadventures. That night at the Shrakes he simply stood around grinning sheepishly and looking downcast, while we all outsported ourselves trying to be amusing.

Sometime that evening I hit upon a wonderful idea. I had just been hired as acting chairman of the SMU Journalism Department, a job that would begin as soon as I got back to the Metroplex. I needed someone with pizazz, who knew what journalism was about, to teach a couple of classes. Not full-time, mind you. Just a couple of classes. Why not, I asked myself, extend the offer to Billie Lee? I recalled what a bang-up impression he made on the student journalists at Texas Tech, and how good the experience had seemed to be for him. His name still had drawing power, at least among people who read books, and I sincerely hoped SMU journalism students read books now and then. Besides, maybe the responsibilities of pedagogy would turn Billie Lee around. I offered him the job. Billie Lee accepted and moved to Dallas within the month.

The journalism program at SMU was at a low ebb when I took over. As a matter of fact, it had been in danger of being discontinued by the liberal arts school when Dean Kermit Hunter of the School of Fine Arts volunteered to take it under his wing. He hired me as interim chairman. To get things rolling, I felt we needed to attract some favorable attention among students, as well as professionals. According to the records I inherited, there were fifteen journalism majors left over from the previous administration. I was able to locate only five of those, and three of the five changed majors that semester. So we were starting from scratch in more ways that one.

My only other faculty member that year was also a part-timer—Peter Gent, who agreed to teach an evening advertising class. Before he became a pass catcher for the Dallas Cowboys, Gent had majored in advertising at Michigan State, where he was an All-America basketball star performer. He had been forced by injuries to retire from pro football and hadn't written *North Dallas Forty* yet. Unlike Billie Lee, Pete was teaching the course strictly as a favor to me. He didn't need the two hundred dollars per month stipend.

For almost the entire school year, Billie Lee (as far as I know) met most of his classes. He was teaching a newswriting lab and a course we had created for upper echelon students wherever we could find them. It was basically a reading and discussion course which attempted to put the students in touch with the responsibilities and rewards of professional journalism. We felt it was inexcusable for a journalism graduate to go into the field without knowing what had been written out there in the real world by the best professionals, and something about the newsmen who were writing the best news media prose, contemporaneously, as well as historically. Later, according to our blueprint, these less than technical aspects of journalism could be incorporated into other courses as they developed. We had to make do with what we had that first year to meet specific student needs the best way we could with limited resources. I had talked with editors at a number of the nation's best newspapers, and they told me they could always teach neophyte journalists to organize a news story and count heads, but news organizations didn't have time to educate them, or to teach them how to write sentences and paragraphs.

As the year got underway, my part-time faculty and I got caught up in the idealism of the job facing us, and the rare opportunity we had to make a difference on the side of the best journalism. I did, anyway, and I think Billie Lee did too, at least for a time. I was commuting from Fort Worth, and most every evening after work I would stop by at either Billie Lee's apartment or Pete and Jody Gent's Oak Lawn home to let the rush hour traffic subside. We exchanged cosmic resolutions to all the world's problems as we listened to the high-impact music that was coming out at that time—Dylan, Rolling Stones, Kris Kristofferson, John Prine, the Beatles, and the Byrds, as well as Buck Owens, and George Jones and others that don't come to mind immediately this far on down the line. Billie Lee's hi-fi system was in hock to the Gents, so we did our listening there.

At SMU, the sixties revolution was apparent essentially in the longer masculine hairstyles and in the thrift shop clothes worn by both males and females. But the students kept up, read underground publications, rejected materialism, hated the war, sneered at Campus Greeks, and expressed the appropriate sentiments in classrooms and certain beer halls near the campus. Something different was happening there, as well as at Berkeley and other campuses in the national news. It was a fascinating time for those of us close enough to cover the story. A time of high hopes for the future. Billie Lee, Pete and I stayed in the background, but in our hearts we empathized with the students. This did not sit well with everybody downtown, of course, or with our dean. Dallas was not exactly famous for its open-mindedness in those days, a fact well-documented in the years since.

Perhaps our most productive teaching sessions that year were impromptu, when Larry King, A. C. Greene, Dwight Sargent (my boss at the *New York Herald Tribune*), Bud Shrake, Ken Kesey, and others dropped by to chat informally with my journalism students, in classroom situations or in my living room after hours.

Word of these extraordinary spontaneous appearances began to spread across the campus, and the journalism department entered upon a renaissance that began attracting some of SMU's better students. Some of those students had majored in journalism previously, as undergraduates, but had ultimately transferred to other departments in disillusionment. By the end of that school year, we had 125 majors and minors signed up for the next fall. I would estimate that at least half that number were seriously considering pursuing careers in the news media and had the talent to accomplish some degree of success in the field. I kept up with most of these kids for a number of years after we all left SMU, and they were (and, no longer kids, still are today) performing gratifyingly well at various newspapers and wire services from Boston to Los Angeles to Alaska. I'm proud of them.

During his first few months at SMU, Billie Lee mentioned Dorothy to me only once. "When Darthy comes back from Mexico," he mumbled one evening on the way to the Gents, "I hope she brings me some heart medicine." You could purchase diet pills in Mexico then without a prescription.

It was a very busy year for me. I was teaching four classes and handling all the departmental paper-shuffling, as well as counseling. I don't know exactly when Billie Lee's determination began to unravel. A couple of times I dispatched a husky pair of varsity football players who were taking journalism classes to ensure that Mr. Brammer got to class on time. Many students were telling me how interesting, and even inspiring, his classes were, but others were complaining that Billie Lee wasn't editing their copy in the newswriting lab. "He just glances at my stories and says, 'Looks fine to me,'" one worried coed told me. I checked into the situation, and soon decided to take over the lab myself for the remainder of the spring semester. By the end of the year, Billie Lee was regularly either missing class altogether or bumbling his way through them.

Shortly before school reconvened the next fall, I could see the handwriting on the wall. The new department chairperson was poised to fire Billie Lee, and I figured it would be best to urge my friend to accept the invitation he had from Bowling Green State University to be writer-in-residence there. In his typically passive manner, Billie Lee allowed Pete and Jody to put him on a plane for Kentucky, although he grumbled all the way to the airport that he'd prefer to stay and teach at SMU. He couldn't seem to grasp the undeniable fact that his beautiful bird's nest on Mockingbird Lane was a thing of the past. A couple of months after he left, I received the following letter:

18 October 1970

El Milmoss:

Well sir ah so goddam and hell I am for a fack right here and have been, more often than not, in respectable thrall of good behavior though fearfully strung out at this instant on account of how else muster up the verbiage and vitality to make these here words on them that paper? Why bother? I say (and there are armies of others, nameless for now, eager to join me in saying) why the fuck not? Possibly to demonstrate once and for most that I by god am still fulsomely and tiresomely capable of self expression communication, myriad epiphanies, occasional prophecy and revelation, and sequential nocturnal emissions—all of it channeled toward and into and sometimes out of old discredited print media. Frens and shameless sycophants may

claim that one is plainly deranged to abandon
stardom as rocky roll equipment manager—yet
I say break wind on such provincial tyrannies!
It by god does a man a bunch of therapeutic
good to at least once or twice a year maybe writing words on yella typish paper. Call me a senti-
mentalist if you will but I say (and I know
somebodies somewheres etc.) a truly full-
blooded man can't sang and dance forever without periodically resorting to phonetic alphabets
of any color persuasion. And of course it's plain
enough is it not? (it is not!) that I'm still pos-
sessed of the old magic. Even now, as I com-
pose, frens and strangers wander past remarking
of mah prose: "How (oddly) lucid! How cogent!
What quaint! Sweet reason! Stupefying imagery!
Damn near coherent. Some gonad! Up his vernacular! Praise the Smith Corona composing Machine!" Etc. I have immortal longings and plan
to go there at Christmas break.

Enclosed find example of famed BGSU daily
J dept fulminations. Very tame, very lame: they
could clearly use a reform administration such
as El Millmoss and his faithful sherpa guide
(whose name, nose and barely recordable height
are disclosed only to precious phar out phew).
We should real and truly get to some such new
assignment as we finish that fancy goddam text-
book you forever dawdling over.

This place is pretty, pleasant, seeming safe
from hippie peril and riot squad assault. Improb-
ably picturesque, in manner of New England
townships: handsome campus, gorgeous under-

grads, impressive post-grad programs here and
there in evidence (though equally common-
place, an astonishing number of impoverished
ones). Enrollment is about 6,000 which is about
twice the population of Bowling Green—a still
pulsing little microcosm that is (for all its su-
perficial pretties) the spit-niffling image of
Anderson's Winesburg, Ohio, grotesques and all.

Most notable aspect at this time is hiatus in
cultural apocalypse, abundant evidence elsewhere . . . it seems four or five years behind
Berkeley; if SMU seems only now evolved into
flower-children, Gentle Thursday concerns but
barely activist syndrome of UT in mid-Sixties.
. . . well Bowling Green is somewhere there at
hootenanny/Kingston Trio stage of . . . . what
the fuck was it? The boys look like Pat Boone
perhaps, two three weeks overdue at the barber
shop. The ladies are rather like Sandra Dee in
miniskirt and training bra. My god I'm suffocat-
ing in all this interminable wholesomeness. The
pitiful kiddies largely drink . . . Indeed, the raging concern at the moment is not grades or demonstrations or elimination of shack-up prohibi-
tions in student housing blah-blah-blah—but
nothing less than the right of students "of age"
(hard stuff for 21 and older; 3.2 beer/wine for
18 and up) to booze it up on campus (that is, in
own rooms and within sanctuaries of fraterni-
ties/sororities.)

Was stunned by cultural (lag) shock first
week here when, heading home after dark across
campus I detected provocative sounds of great

masses of people stomping and sanging and raising some sort of radical new left queer commie
hell . . . Except I kept hearing ukuleles! How
the fuck them anachronistic muzak pickers?
Also, loudly and clearly now as I moved closer,
these protesting voices seemed directed at one
of the larger lady dorms. And so help me Jesus
there it was: a genuine pantie raid: mobs of
randy crewcut future FBI agents and cybernetic
slavies whooping and moaning for lady under-
wear (pantie girdles accepted). . . . The fuzz gathered on the periphery of this astonishing turnout
were vaguely reminiscent of Marine assault
troopers advised at last moment that nuclear
devices shall henceforth be tested on every
motherfucker everywhere including Joint
Cheese and inter-cervix rivals who look re-
motely smartass.

Still, these nice cleanwashed shorthair nip-
pers are intelligent, reasonably competent as
writers, more or less sophisticated (in baroque
ways, such as obsessions with modern jazz, V.
Nabokov and Wm. Burroughs, little or no interest in Hemingway or A. Ginchburgh) soccer, ice
skating, homecoming (homecoming?), such
radicalism as has yet been apparent is vaguely
anti-establishment (because of Kent State much
more than Fred Hampton or Jackson State, etc.)
not so much anti-war and anti-draft, not so much
pro Democrat (or left of anywhere) as perhaps
profoundly disappointed in Nixon, Mitchell, etc.
Kunstler provoked an astonishing turnout of the
ex-Mickey Mousketeers, and wisely thumped

away on the raw nerve of the Administration's all-out war on college students all over. This appeal to their own immediate paranoia was in fact only real responsive emotion apparent in course of his pitch . . . One wonders if they are capable of declaring (not a separate peace) but a separate war on straight old-timer society, clearly distinct from any such dope-crazed guerrilla theater shit or Weatherman terrorism one normally associates with student activism. These kids are going to mount the barricades, win the fucking revolution, then split quickly for hometowns thruout Middle West where they will usurp and seize banks, buildings, stores and Cadillac dealerships once in clutches of their old men.

Booze—Oh Jesus yes: weekends look like fraternity row in Austin at Roundup. But the hippie community, in and out of school, probably couldn't muster sufficient numbers for a Kappa Sig chapter. The local head shop, beautiful little place well stocked with psychedelic posters and Sgt. Pepper field jacks, well, so help me, this place doesn't even stock Zig Zag papers!

Ah but I digress. I had only meant to say hidy and assure anyone who cares that I am unimaginable well-liked here and can't wait to get home to my frens, rocky-roll music, beloved Poodle dog and (reassure me endlessly!) grabass teaching career. I am ever your fawning subordinate and Rotter in Residence.

Billie Lee
Rising Gorge, Ont.

I've been involved in a bunch of projects through the years. Some turned out better than others and some were more fun than others, but none was ever quite like the SMU melodrama. When perspective returned, I realized I never had anything turn out as well as that endeavor. Even the idea of getting Billie Lee up there wasn't all bad, nor was it unsuccessful. I personally know of three students who were inspired by Billie Lee to read their first books. That alone is worth a lot, even though Billie Lee's going in and out of focus on me was trying from time to time.

There weren't nearly as many published authors living and working in Texas back then as there are now. New York and California were still a long way from Texas and still held a monopoly on big league success in the letters. Billie Lee was a Texan, living in Texas, who had defined Texas in a unique way, and his prose style had been accepted as engaging and authentic by the biggest of the big leaguers on both coasts. Other Texas writers who were still around were old men who wrote about old times. Or lived somewhere else and probably looked like college professors. Billie Lee was our Norman Mailer. Quiet, yes, but he was out there amongst 'em. In the early-to-middle sixties, if you went anywhere that was anywhere, you ran into Billie Lee Brammer talk.

For a long time after Billie Lee died, every time a bunch of us got together, somebody would always say something like: "Let's make a pledge: No Billie Lee stories tonight. After this one. . . ." One story inevitably would be followed by just one more, which would be followed by another and another and, before we could stop ourselves, we would have spent another entire evening regaling each other with Billie Lee stories, while others at the party hooked up with every single one of the fascinating damsels present. We would curse ourselves for foolishly falling into that predicament yet again and solemnly vow never again to be so reckless. And we stuck to our oaths. Until the next time. They were amusing stories, but I guess you had to know Billie Lee to fully appreciate most of them. Like the day Susan Walker and I walked in on Billie Lee and found him dancing alone to reggae music. You had to know him to understand how remarkably Billie Lee-ish that was. We watched him dance alone for maybe fifteen minutes before he noticed we were there.

He was one of the most passive-appearing human beings, male or female, I've ever known. On the other hand, he would always fall in with just about any of the shockingly imaginative and outrageous plans for mischief some of the best literary minds in America could concoct. He was a walking (and sitting and lying down) contradiction, just like a couple of other guys Kristofferson (one of Billie Lee's favorite poets) sang about—Billy Swann and Jerry Jeff Walker, and maybe Johnny Cash. He hadn't even met Billie Lee when he wrote that song, but he probably did meet him somewhere further on down the line.

Everybody else did—or so it seemed. Billie Lee was one of those folks everybody wanted to meet as soon as they heard about him, one by one, for their own reasons, whatever they might have been. After meeting him, for some reason, most people sooner or later developed an urge to mother Billie Lee. Especially women, but not just womankind. All of his cronies seemed to go out of their way to please him. He had that effect on you. You just felt obliged to indulge him. He was so . . . so civilized.

You had to lean in to hear him, he spoke so softly. And it wasn't always easy to follow Billie Lee's train of thought. But if you tried hard, it was inevitably well worth the trouble. He had always read everything you had read, in addition to everything you intended to read. He was familiar with every album you intended to buy when you got around to it. He had already gotten around to it somehow.

He was always up on the latest gossip, too. All the latest goings-on rumored about rocks stars and famous authors and the latest scandals about his very own dearly beloved friends. Another Billie Lee theory was that he concocted much of the gossip himself—made it up entirely or punched it up a bit. You suspected as much, but somehow Billie Lee managed to pull it off and make you a believer. It was as if you understood in some way that he only exaggerated to amuse you by telling you something you didn't already know. Billie Lee could be wide-eyed innocence personified, with one hand lifting your wallet. Or your pills.

Back then almost everybody had their stash of diet pills. Secretaries swallowed them with their orange juice. On-the-go, up-and-coming executives of all persuasions popped them to keep up with the competition. It wasn't speed; they were only Diet Pills. It was like you were the only one who knew they gave you an edge. Distinguished believers in the Hippocratic oath got ever richer and richer dispensing prescriptions for the little boogers, and there was no warning on the label. Stealing pills from each other's medicine cabinets became a common compulsion. Merely a misdemeanor. Everyone was doing it, but only about half were trying to keep it a secret. It wasn't against the law to buy or sell those pills then. Nobody had mentioned the dangers. Flip-outs were blamed on other things—like a fundamental weakness of character. Most people claimed they could take them or leave them. Others found they could not. Billie Lee could not.

When Gary Cartwright was living at the J. Frank Dobie Ranch one year, he and his wife, Jo, had a party out there. The place was packed with writers, musicians, several fairly well-known actors (including Howard Hessman who had been in Bud Shrake's movie *Kid Blue* in Mexico earlier that summer), various strays, and no telling who all. The soiree went on for several days and nights. At its peak, Shrake and a Hollywood producer by the name of Marvin Schwartz (John Wayne's *War Wagon*) furtively followed Billie Lee around and every time he struck up a conversation, they would put a stop watch on him to time how long it would take him to hit up whoever he was chatting with for pills. Best I recall, the longest interval they noted was twenty-three seconds.

Why did Billie Lee choose being high over fulfilling his potential? Nobody really knows, of course, although the question was pondered endlessly by those who knew him well and many who barely knew him at all. Billie Lee's first marriage broke up about the time *The Gay Place* came out in 1961. A little before or a little after. He was reticent about his personal feelings most of the time, but he had spells of talking about himself and his problems. One night Billie Lee told me he was afraid to write another book because he didn't know how. At the time he confessed this to me, he was still the toast of Austin. Maybe that's what he was hiding from. Or maybe not. Billie Lee perhaps agreed with Johnny Cash who, when asked if he took diet pills for this or that deep psychological reason, said he took them because he liked the way they made him feel.

Even after he gave up trying to keep up a reasonable front, there was a charismatic aura about Billie Lee. You got the feeling that he knew something you didn't know, and that if you could make friends with him, he might share some of those secrets with you. Even though Billie Lee was not a Life-of-the-Party type, party-seekers seemed to gravitate to him. Back when he was still trying to write, drunken pals used to come by Billie Lee's place after the bars shut down at midnight. Closing time at Scholz's and other Austin hang-outs for politicians and political groupies frequently produced someone on a roll who was likely to say, "Let's go over to ole Billie Lee's. He's always up." And he undoubtedly was.

Edwin (Bud) Shrake, Pied Piper of Wildcat Hollow

I don't have to stay up all night anymore, like I often used to think I did. There's nothing out there after dark I think I want. But once upon a time, if it was a party, I was there. Along with most other card-carrying Maddogs. We've been known to drive hundreds of miles just to be there. As many times as I've tried to figure out the reason for this, I've never come up with a really plausible answer. Except maybe one: we were hoping, maybe even eagerly anticipating, that tonight would be the night IT would happen.

"IT" was never exactly defined, as far as I know, but probably had something to do with women. (Or, for female Maddogs, men.) Maybe this would be the night I would meet that certain extraordinary Woman, the one who would see who I really was, who the ME really was inside this more or less ordinary body and behind this more or less ordinary face and demeanor.

On the other hand, this might be the night somebody said something that opened wide all those doors in my mind that stubbornly had kept me from knowing all those important, vital things that I didn't know, but were known by so many others. Either or both such possibilities were well worth giving it one more try. And I can say with conviction that I did do that. Give it a try, that is.

For instance, one night Bud Shrake and I left somebody's house in Fort Worth where a small party had been going on and headed for Austin at well past midnight. Our reasoning went something like this: Nothing interesting was happening in Fort Worth, but something really preposterous was probably happening in Austin, since there nearly always was, so we would motor on down to Austin forthwith.

Well, it was rather late and our minds were somewhat scrambled, so when we got to the traffic circle that used to be on the main highway going through Waco, we came out on the wrong road and wound up going quite a distance off course, kind of kitty-cornered away from Austin, until we came to some little town we knew, even in our scrambled minds, was not on the way to Austin and made a mid-course navigational correction, so that eventually we did indeed wind up in the capital city of the Lone Star State.

By that time, however, the sun had been up for some time and we couldn't find anyone to play with. We had a lot of phones rudely slammed down in our ears by close personal friends, and our feelings were hurt. So, we went to Scholz's Garten to lick our wounds and soothe our sensitive souls with a cold beer or two.

Sure enough, it wasn't long before a familiar face came into view. The familiar face was that of John, a young man from Amarillo, a university student we had known for some time who, we agreed, was undoubtedly natural Maddog material, even though I think this all happened before Maddog, Inc. was formally founded, or established, or whatever.

John introduced us to the young lady with him and announced that inasmuch as she was pregnant, they were getting married that very afternoon, as soon as his family and some friends arrived from Amarillo. In a burst of generosity, John told us we should, if we hadn't already registered at a hotel, hustle right over to the Villa Capri Motel where the wedding party was staying and tell the man at the desk we were part of the wedding party and our rooms would be paid for by his father. Which we did—*post haste.*

By noon, we had decided to throw a party for our good friends, John and his bride, so we called everybody we could think of and invited them to our rooms at the inn. We ordered food and beverages from room service and told the innkeeper to put it on our bill. When the time for the actual nuptials arrived, quite a festive celebration had developed. I seem to remember seeing Darrell Royal and some of his assistant coaches there, along with most of the people who would one day be card-carrying Maddogs.

The next day, back at Scholz's, we ran into John. He said his father had asked him after the ceremony where we were. He called us, "Those nice boys who gave you that swell party before the wedding."

I didn't meet anybody extraordinary on that trip, nor did I learn any amazing secrets about life its ownself (as Dan Jenkins might put it). I don't think I even had a whole lot of fun. But that didn't keep me from trying again. And again. As often as not with Bud Shrake.

Like that fellow who lured the mice and children out of Hamlin, Shrake had a way about him that persuaded people to do things they might not ordinarily do. Shrake was a notorious promoter of "Nekkid Bridge" tournaments, for example. Losers of each game had to remove an article of clothing.

Shrake touted Nekkid Bridge most enthusiastically when there were one or two exceptionally good looking women in the group—especially good looking women who hadn't played bridge that much. Ironically—at least sometimes I considered it so, and at other times I suspected it might have been cleverly planned—the master bridge player, Shrake, often wound up nekkid his ownself instead of the exceptionally good looking woman in question. Of course, that could have been because he lost his concentration. But that's a topic for debate at another time and place. We are concerned here with more serious matters. Like Shrake's uncanny ability to somehow manage to get his writing accomplished even when he was staying up all night, every night, with the rest of us.

I've tried and I've tried, but I've never been able to figure out when Shrake managed to find the clear-headed time to write, but he has, somehow, turned out several better-than-average novels, at least two best-selling "as told to" books and had a couple of his stage plays produced, along with several screenplays for television and the big screen.

The picker poets I could understand. They didn't get off work until 2:00 A.M., and had to unwind. But they did a lot of their songwriting while they were working, as well as after work in the wee, small hours of the morning, when they were still wired from performing and gathered in smoky rooms with their guitars and a small crowd of admirers to cheer them on. Prose writers don't usually operate that way.

In the middle sixties, Shrake was widely known, both as a personage and as a writer, in Dallas, Fort Worth and surrounding communities, where he was a semi-legendary sports columnist and *bon vivant* before moving to Manhattan to write for *Sports Illustrated* and help his Fort Worth Paschal High and TCU mate, Dan Jenkins, make places like Elaine's and P. J. Clarke's famous as hangouts for writers and actors—just as they had done for Joe T. Garcia's (Mexican food in Fort Worth), Massey's (Fort Worth's famous chicken-fried steak and cream gravy place) and Pete Dominguez's Casa Dominguez (Mexican food in Dallas), and others.

When Ann Richards was governor of Texas, Shrake squired her various places, such as inaugural balls, Jerry Jeff Walker recording sessions and live performances on Austin City Limits, as well as visits to the Dallas Cowboys summer workout camp site in Austin, occasional movies and University of Texas basketball games. When television and press cameras caught them together at such events, Texans in some parts of the state would wonder, "Who's that tall fellow with our lady governor?" That tall fellow was Bud Shrake—a lanky six feet, five inches or so.

Veterans of the Austin social scene didn't have to ask. They knew Shrake, or knew about him, and probably had heard more than a few "Shrake tall tales." For a number of years, he was a running buddy of such notorious Austinites as Willie Nelson, Jerry Jeff Walker, Darrell Royal and Gary Cartwright.

Austin has always loved rumors, so it was inevitable that tales would circulate speculating that Governor Ann and Shrake were headed for marriage. Both parties denied these stories. The governor went so far as to tell one reporter the only man she would consider marrying would be rich and "on a life support system." Shrake didn't qualify on either count.

He's hopefully a long way from needing life support systems, but Shrake, like most other Maddogs of old, has altered his lifestyle drastically. Larry L. King keeps up with most Maddogs from the old days, although he, too, has turned into a relatively tame homebody. As long ago as 1991, King wrote that he'd been in Austin to make a speech and visited awhile with Shrake.

"Bud's working real hard," King wrote. "Jody Gent, who works for him now and then, says his routine these days is unvarying: he gets up and plays golf, comes back from golf and takes a shower and puts on his jammies and house slippers and writes all day.

"Just like you and me and the other former dancing fools who now get our kicks watching Vanna turn letters on the TV," King went on, "Bud don't ever go out at night any more."

No doubt, King's report was something of an exaggeration to make a point, as it was written about the same time Shrake was photographed at various events with Governor Richards. But it was a point well worth making, for several reasons, both pertinent and interesting to a fellow Maddog, like myself, who sometimes thinks I'm the only former party animal who gives up and goes to bed, often as not, before the "adult" prime time TV shows come on.

It was not always thus. There was a time when (as Shrake himself put it to a *Dallas Morning News* reporter doing a story on Texas's "First Boyfriend"), "if there was a party, I was at it."

For example, there was the time when the party consisted of Shrake, Fletcher and Jean Boone and myself, and we decided to motor down to Laredo on the border to see a bull fight. Shrake drove most of the way down and, because he was working on a novel, he instructed me, riding in the back seat, to take notes as he called them out. My notes later appeared almost verbatim in his novel, *But Not for Love*, a deed for which I took full credit in a speech I made in Shrake's place at a luncheon meeting of the Fort Worth Friends of the Library. I read for the Library Friends this passage, which I pointed out came straight from my notes:

And always there were the signs on the highway:
HONOR ALL
and
THE KINGDOM OF GOD IS AT HAND
and
BURMA SHAVE
IF YOU DRIVE, DON'T DRINK.

After the luncheon Shrake's mother came up to me, thanked me for filling in for her son, Edwin (who was on some assignment for *Sports Illustrated* and had called me only the night before to inform me he had told the program chairperson I had agreed to give a talk to the Friends of the Library in his stead) and with a very serious look on her face, asked, "Don't you think Bud could write a nice book if he really tried?"

I agreed with Mrs. Shrake I thought he probably could. If he really tried.

To tell the honest truth, our entire Laredo escapade turned out to be a big disappointment—from the bullfight to the night life. From our seats in the rickety arena plastered with peeling bullfight posters, we watched the scrawny, skinny-legged star matador with a big, ugly patch on the seat of his faded satin suit of lights waggle his cape, as he nervously awaited the charge of an equally scrawny, skinny-legged bull. It was pitiful. Eventually, the picadors had to slay *El Toro* by bludgeoning him to death and dragging him from the dusty arena in a stream of gore. The forlorn teenage bullfighter had missed all the essential points with his swords. My fellow fun seekers and I solemnly viewed these festive proceedings as an off-key brass band played its accompanying fanfare. A Hemingway-esque spectacle the bullfight was not, and it set the tone for our adventure-filled Mexican holiday.

That evening, our guide escorted us to a Laredo nightclub. The *senoritas* there weren't exactly candidates for Miss
Universe, but they would dance with you if you bought them
a beer. Fletcher expressed his admiration of me as an irresistible ladies man until he discovered I had been buying the
ladies cervezas to get them to favor me with a dance. This
discovery was upsetting to Fletcher because I was the one
designated by the group to carry our money for the trip. To
my amazement, the honorable office of chancellor of the ex-
chequer was snatched away from me immediately and
awarded instead to Fletcher's wife, the famous TV star, Jean
Boone, whom he trusted not to frivolously spend our trip
money buying beer for young ladies.

Later, we made a half-hearted run at Laredo's Boy's Town,
but found it was against the rules to bring into the area a
female "outsider." Unwanted competition, no doubt, banned
by the *jefes* of the girls in the cribs and nightclubs. By that
time, we were all set to argue that this was a blatant violation
of anti-trust laws, but were reminded that Anglo laws did not
apply across the border, which of course, was exactly why we
were there in the first place.

During the afternoon and early evening, between the bullfight and the nightclub dancing, we were shown the town by
our guide, Jesus, who wore what he proudly claimed to be a
police uniform. He told us he was a genuine policeman, duly
appointed by his cousin, the *Jefe* of the *Policia*, but just as a
sideline, he worked as a tourist guide. Jesus was a loyal and
attentive escort, and as a matter of fact, later sent cards to
both Shrake and Fletcher asking for money and declaring he
would work for them if allowed to cross the border to Texas.

As most Texans were, our party was well aware one could
purchase prescription drugs in Mexico without prescriptions
(in those days, anyhow). This applied to the ever-popular diet

pills, such as Dexamil, Dexedrine and dexa-anything else. As a good many citizens before us, we had discovered that in addition to stifling one's hunger pangs, those diet pills could keep one awake all night and sometimes, if one was very determined and had an adequate supply, for several nights in a row. Business men and women from Wall Street to Lubbock were arising each morning and swallowing at least one diet pill to get their motors running quicker and faster and longer— to compete with all the other men and women who were doing the same thing. Professional football players and other athletes lined up regularly before game time to get their "energy" pills from trainers. Some teams were allowing sports writers in to the energy pill line along with the players. At least, that's what I heard from some sports writers I knew.

Sometime before the light of dawn, we decided we should motor on down to Monterrey, a small city in the Mexican state of Nuevo Leon, far enough from the border to be more Mexican, with less border town ambiance and therefore, a more satisfying place to visit for a group of intellectually-minded artistic types such as my traveling companions and myself. Fortified with an abundant supply of energy pills, we made the drive to Monterrey in good speed, arriving in time for the afternoon siesta. By that time, however, our respective bloodstreams awash with the dexa-whatever in our recently purchased Mexican diet pills, none of us was able to relax for even a short nap.

I thought a hot shower might help, but found the water from the shower in my motel room was only a lukewarm dribble. I pretended for awhile that I was enjoying a bona fide shower, but eventually gave that up as a futile exercise. I got dressed and went for a walk in a nearby plaza where I found Shrake reclining upon a park bench, seemingly in a thoughtful mood.

"Welcome to Monterrey," I said, plopping down beside him. Soon, we were joined by Mr. Boone, who said Jean had succeeded in coaxing enough water from their faucet to bathe and was at that moment either asleep or pretending to be. So, the three of us put our feverish brains together and came up with a plan.

We moved from the park to a bar in one of the nicer hotels and soon met this friendly fellow who told us he was editor of a local magazine aimed at tourists. When we told him we were accompanied by a big TV star from Texas, Miss Jean Boone, he asked if he could interview her and maybe get a few photos for his next edition. We assured the friendly fellow that, although she was in Mexico to rest from her intense schedule, we could persuade Miss Boone to cooperate.

By that time the bar will filling up gradually with well dressed men and women. I was elected (I forget now what I was being punished for; probably my aforementioned cerveza buying indiscretions) to walk back to our hotel and let Miss Boone in on our plan. I was to tell her to dress appropriately in TV star fashion and meet us in the hotel bar.

Before I left to pass the message to Jean, I gave Shrake specific instructions to pick up two beautiful young Mexican señoritas—one for me and one for him, and it would be a bonus if they were unable to speak or understand English. He promised to do so. Told me not to worry, he was a man whose word was his bond, a handshake was as good as a contract, and all that kind of stuff. So, I left on my chore with a light heart, certain that when I returned, I would be greeted by a lovely young Mexican princess who would address me as "Meester Meelner" in a sweet, respectful voice and who would soon, no doubt, be overwhelmed by my Anglo charm.

I hurried back from my errand and, from the bar doorway, saw two reasonably pretty young women sitting at the

table with Shrake and Fletcher and our new friend, the magazine editor. When I was introduced, I noticed right away, however, that the ladies spoke English. They not only spoke
English, but spoke it with decidedly Texas accents. The two
turned out to be secretaries from Houston who had come down
on their vacation for the annual pigeon shoot, to be held that
week in Monterrey.

"Pigeon shoot groupies, eh?" I aimed the question at Shrake,
along with a fierce glare I hoped carried all the complexities
of my feelings at the moment. He answered with a shrug that
seemed to me to convey the message, "A bird in hand . . ." or
some such nonsense.

The Houston secretaries giggled prettily.

To make a long (very long) story short enough to hold
your interest, after the friendly magazine editor snapped a
few photographic poses of Jean in her TV star get-up, we
motored across the mountain to the town of Saltillo, further
inland and therefore, we figured, even more authentically
Mexican. Shrake and I, being your basic optimists, invited
the Houston secretaries to accompany us on our Saltillo expedition. On the way, we tried to turn on what we confidently
considered to be our not inconsiderable wit and charm in
order to overwhelm their conspicuous indifference, but were
noticeably unsuccessful. The ladies didn't even fall for our
usually infallible ploy, perfected at numerous parties in Dallas and Austin, and Fort Worth: Shrake would request that I
sing the old Ernest Tubb classic, "Percy Wilson Gay," and I, in
turn, would request that Shrake render his impression of Richard Burton impersonating Winston Churchill.

When even that tried and true scheme failed to arouse the
interest of the Houston secretaries, it wasn't hard to convince
Fletcher and Jean it was time for us all to head for home. We
were bone weary and irritable during the long drive back to

the border. The Houston secretaries had driven their own car, so we were able to take a short-cut, bypassing Monterrey.

Most of the trip back to the border was made in grumpy silence, punctuated by an occasional attempt by one of us to concoct some elaborate scheme or another to bravely smuggle our diet pill stash into Texas. The closer we got to the border, the more irritable and nervous we became, as Fletcher described increasingly grim scenarios depicting the three of us locked up in a filthy Mexican jail for the rest of our lives, which wouldn't be very long due to the inhumane, if not tortuous treatment we would surely receive there, perpetrated upon us not only by the swarthy desperadoes who would share our miserable cells, but by the bloodthirsty Mexican jailers also, all of whom would be clones of the toothy bandit who stole Bogart's shoes in *The Treasure of the Sierra Madre*. No matter how sensitive and liberal one may be, stereotypes, apparently, are hard to shake loose.

By the time we had, at last, crossed the border and were safely back in Texas, we had peevishly tossed all the pills out the car windows except (we later learned) three that Fletcher had hidden in the cuff of his pants. Naturally, none of us ever told (until now, of course, when it no longer matters) what we had done—or not done. The truth might have tarnished our reputations as dashing outlaws.

This was all back in 1962, not long after I returned to Texas from my hitches on the *New York Post* and the *New York Herald Tribune*. Shrake was writing his column for the *Dallas Morning News* sports section at that time. He not only gleaned material for two columns from our Mexico trip, but later put his version in his novel, *But Not For Love,* the one in which he used my notes, you know. Shrake's version turned out quite different than mine, but then he was writing fiction, and my version of the story is factual. Well, as factual as I am able to recall it at this late date. If Fletcher and Jean remember it differently, that's their story.

Fletcher did no painting or sculpting during those squandered Mexico days, and I did no writing. But Shrake somehow was able to sneak in two columns and one chapter of his novel. I guess it has something to do with endurance, determination, and maybe something beyond strength of character. I've given it considerable thought, and the only conclusion I've been able to reach is that it has mostly to do with lack of shame. Guilt can squeeze off one's creative juices, as sure as anything; so vicey versey: lack of guilt must leave one free to create up a storm, regardless of one's actions away from his or her art. And the only other person I've ever known personally, the only other creative artist, I should say, who was less burdened by guilt or shame than Shrake, regardless of what outrageous thing he might have done or tried to do the night or the week before, was Jerry Jeff Walker, whose robust freedom from shame was greatly admired by Shrake himself.

Shrake once told me a story about Jerry Jeff and remorse. He told it proudly, so I knew he envied his picker poet friend. Shrake and Jerry Jeff had recognized each other almost immediately as soul mates when they first met. Shrake asked Jerry Jeff (he usually called him Jackie Jack, as did many others who admired Walker's ability to endure free from penitence), "Don't you ever feel any remorse?" This was one day after the singer/songwriter had worn out numerous drinking buddies over a period of several days and nights, and wound up at an all-night pornographic book and video store where he had invited all the customers there to come home with him and go swimming in his pool.

"See, what you do," Jerry Jeff answered without hesitation, "is you pour your blender full of orange juice and put about a dozen B-12 pills in there and run the blender until it's all well mixed, and then you drink it down, and if the law hasn't stopped in your driveway by that time and the phone isn't ringing off the wall, you know you've pulled it off."

As time went by, we grew less cautious about indulging in the chaotic whims and obsessions of the sixties. After Ken Kesey and his Merry Pranksters took their famous bus trip, stopping briefly to visit with Larry McMurtry at his Houston home, the next step inevitably was to try an Electric Kool Aid acid test ourselves. To find out where it took you and what it did to you there. We were, after all, *arteests*, and had to be out there on the cutting edge.

So, one day Shrake called from Dallas and said it was my turn—that we would meet that evening at the apartment of this Dallas banker friend, who was already well ahead of us, and they would all watch over me as I went on A Trip.

"Of course, I'll be there," I said, my hand steady and my voice firm. "I'm no chicken." But the several hours between that phone call from Shrake and LSD-time were enough for me to think about it, and think about it I did. This was early enough in that era that we hadn't heard a lot of the horror stories we would hear later, so it was mainly a vague anxiety like the dread of taking a plunge into something unknown but not necessarily fearsome. I was glad when the time came and the drive to Dallas was done. Shrake and Cartwright were there, along with Jim Smithum, a friend through Jean and Fletcher we all liked to talk with who had read nearly everything. Pete and Jody Gent and the banker, of course, were also there and a couple others whose names and faces don't immediately pop up on my mental Rolodex at the moment.

The banker was a collector of books and records. His living room was full of them, floor to ceiling and wall to wall. He placed a Bob Dylan album on the stereo—(I don't recall the album title but it was the one with "Stuck Inside a Mobile" and I later understood the words for the first time)—then he stood the album jacket up in front of one of the speakers. The face of Bob Dylan was life size or larger, in some kind of sparkledy 3-D that made Dylan appear to wink and wave at you as he sang his surreal lyrics. All this was before I even swallowed the tiny pill.

I forget what color the pill was because I think I closed my eyes as I took it from the banker's fingers and transferred it to my mouth and swallowed. I remember thinking: "I don't really want to do this," but by then it was too late. That's one thing about LSD that anyone considering trying it should keep foremost in mind: Once you swallow it, there's no going back. You are on your way to somewhere, somewhere that might turn out to be scary, very scary, or very interesting, or—more likely—both.

To this day I remember more of the details of that acid trip than one might think. I remember at least once having to be called back by my friends who were watching and who somehow realized my mind was heading in a dangerous direction, or at best, a direction that would carry me to a place I intensely didn't want to be. I no longer remember where I was heading when they called me back, but I do remember being very grateful for the rescue.

I can still remember quite clearly that I saw and understood that everything is connected to everything else. Everything and everybody, and even every animal and every plant, all harmoniously linked and somehow amicably related. I clearly saw all that and totally understood it, although I couldn't for the life of me explain it to you now.

And I saw the history of the United States in narrative form, all the characters speaking their lines clearly, from the Revolutionary War through the Great Depression. General Washington and his aides plotting the battle at Valley Forge,

FDR discussing how to restructure our government so more people would have jobs to buy food for their families. It was all so crystal clear, I tried to explain to Jim Smithum. He smiled and nodded as if he understood, and that pleased me.

Later, after I had come back to the present in my mind, I said to Smithum: "Wasn't that fascinating, that condensed history of the United States I told you?"

"Do you know what you were saying to me?" Smithum asked cruelly. "You said, 'Ogg ogg ogg ogg.'"

"Then why were you nodding as if you understood?" I asked foolishly. "Because I didn't want to upset you," he answered wisely.

● ● ●

My contacts with Shrake are rare these days. In point of fact, I confess I don't socialize with any of the old Maddog gang anymore—except my wife, Gail, who earned her Maddog status and official membership card soon after we were married in 1983. Gail was immediately recognized as a natural Maddog by none other than Susan Walker, who knows a Maddog when she sees one, if anyone ever did. Susan, a Maddog in her own right, has lived with a Maddog for more than twenty years and has had them coming in and out her doors longer than that.

It's not that my Maddog wife and I feel we have outgrown our former Maddog playmates or anything like that. We simply don't wander out at night much anymore. Nor do they, I hear. People change, of course, but it's not easy to visualize Bud Shrake in a rocking chair, shawl about his shoulders, watching *Wheel of Fortune* before slipping off to bed. If he does, indeed, stay home every evening, it's a safe bet he's thinking bawdy thoughts.

The truth is, by staying home, getting plenty of rest and exercise, and spending all that time at his keyboard, Shrake may well be writing something that will leave a permanent mark on the literary world, and I don't mean just the Texas literary world. Bud Shrake might be the best writer in the bunch that bridged the gap between J. Frank Dobie and his gang and the Texans who are writing all kinds of books these days in almost every corner of the state.

He's always had the talent and the necessary keen eyes, ears and philosophical perception to be regarded among the best America has had to offer. Shrake's problem (if, indeed, you can truly call it a problem, since it boils down more to a choice than any lack of anything missing and, of course, this is my personal assessment and not the word of God) is that over the years, Shrake chose not to isolate himself for the long periods of time it takes to create quote Literature un-quote. Even so, he has come close a time or two. But—there's probably more money in screenplays and TV movies and guaranteed bestsellers such as ghostwritten biographies of Willie Nelson and Barry Switzer.

Larry McMurtry, who has turned out a bushel basket of novels and books of essays, earned a Pulitzer Prize, and seri-ously competed for a passle of other literary and film awards, told me several years ago he sometimes regretted the isola-tion required to do all that writing, and often felt he had missed out on a lot.

I doubt, on the other hand, that Shrake seriously regrets his Maddog years.

Jay Milner's football photo from the Lubbock High School yearbook, 1942–43.

J. D. MILNER
Guard—Weight 177
One of the toughest and roughest guards in the history of Lubbock High School.

Jay Milner. (Photo by Jay Brakefield, Milner's grandson.)

Billy Lee Brammer, around 1966.

Larry L. King and SMU
journalism student Don
Hunter in 1970.

Bud Shrake at SMU film festival in 1971 that featured his movie, *Kid Blue*, starring Dennis Hopper.

(left to right) Jay Milner, Billy Swann, Billy Joe Shaver and Jerry Jeff Walker backstage at Old Castle Creek, Austin, 1973.

Professor Jay Milner (glasses and no jacket) is greeted by some of his SMU journalism students after they won all student writing prizes but one at a regional meeting of SDX, a professional journalism society, in Hot Springs, Arkansas, in 1971. Behind Milner are professional newsmen who were there to see the action.

Columnist Joe Murray and a few of his dogs. (Photo by Jay Milner)

Jay Milner, Geno McCoslin and Willie Nelson at Milner's birthday party at McCoslin's Dallas night club, 57 Doors, in 1973. (Photo by Chuck Gist)

Gary Cartwright singing the song he and Bud Shrake wrote for Jay Milner's 1973 birthday party, with accompanist Willie Nelson.

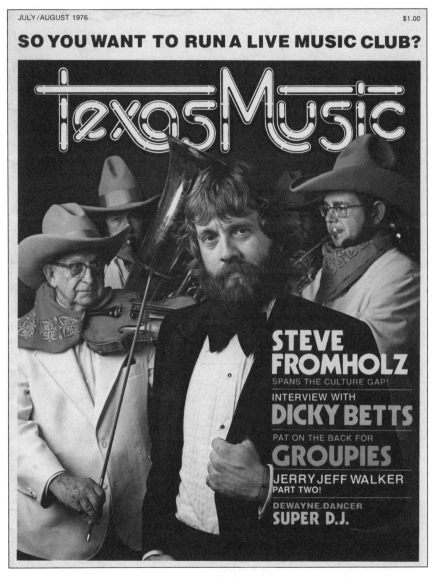

The cover of one of the few issues of *Texas Music* magazine.

Jerry Jeff Walker and Bud Shrake, taken at Jerry Jeff's surprise birthday party in Austin, 1975. (Photo by Cookie DeShay)

Willie Nelson (right) with Jay Milner (in hat) in Dallas radio studio in 1976 promoting an upcoming 4th of July Picnic. The DJ is Steve Kaufman, who played only Texas music on his highly popular show. (Photo by Ron McKeown)

Bud Shrake (in cap), Libby Boone, Fletcher Boone and Jerry Jeff Walker chat after Jay and Gail's wedding in 1983. (Photo by Marieta Boyle)

The groom and bride chat with Gary Cartwright following the wedding. (Photo by Marieta Boyle)

Susan Walker, Gail and Jay Milner at the Walker home in Austin following the Milner wedding there in 1983. Susan Walker was not only hostess of the wedding and reception but served as Jay's "Best Person." (Photo by Marieta Boyle)

Literary Giants and William Randolph Hearse

In 1961, Bud Shrake, Gary Cartwright and Dan Jenkins were still dazzling Dallas with their literate, humorous coverage of college and professional sports (they didn't see athletics as the most important struggle in the world). This was back before there were Mavericks and Rangers, so the Metroplex was essentially a one-professional sports community, not counting soccer and most folks didn't. That one sport was, of course, Dallas Cowboys football. The Texans had moved to Kansas City. Shrake and Cartwright had severed ties with their long-time mentor and editor, Blackie Sherrod at the *Times Herald*, and had gone over to the *Morning News*, where Shrake's daily column now ran down the left-hand side of the sports section page one, in direct competition with Sherrod's popular, prize-winning column in the *Times-Herald*. That rivalry was the topic of conversation at every gathering for awhile. Shrake and Cartwright were looked upon by their many hard-core fans as high-spirited rebels with a cause. The exact nature of their rebellious cause was not all that clear, but whatever it was, or wasn't, it seemed to be full of compassion and fun, as all really admirable causes are or ought to be. A few years later, when I was teaching journalism, I was struck by the number of my students who had been lured into the profession as high school kids by the dash and style of the Dallas sportswriters of that era. It is unlikely that any other city has ever enjoyed so much excellent sports writing as Dallas and its environs did when Sherrod, Jenkins, Cartwright and Shrake were all there at the same time.

Meantime, in Texas letters, J. Frank Dobie was still the king, and people still read Roy Bedichek. Larry L. King was working for a congressman. William A. Owens was on the faculty at Columbia University. A. C. Greene was (depending on the year) putting out the editorial page, book page, and Op-Ed page at the *Times-Herald*, which was the most interesting local daily in Texas at the time, unless it was the *Corpus Christi Caller-Times*, and from time to time Fort Worth's under-financed *Press*.

Billie Lee's friend Larry McMurtry (they both went to North Texas at different times, or something like that), was around Austin now and then in the 1960s, the early Brammer period. He would show up for a few days, then disappear for months at a time. Somebody said they thought he was teaching English composition at TCU, and playing pool against his students on the varsity football team to determine their grades. We found out later that when McMurtry disappeared, he was writing. A few years later, when he was teaching at Rice, he came out with his second novel, *Leaving Cheyenne*. I got a call from Bud Shrake the week I read it. All he said was "Have you read McMurtry's new one?" I said I had, and Shrake said "Don't it make you want to cry because you didn't write it?" and I said yes, it did, indeed.

Shrake was calling from Houston, where he was covering something for *Sports Illustrated*. He said he had started reading *Leaving Cheyenne* on the plane down, then finished it that night before going out to a party, where he was surprised and pleased to see McMurtry. He called a cab and went back to his hotel to get his copy of the new book so the author could sign it. He said McMurtry took the volume to a corner and sat there for a long time, apparently pondering over what to write. Shrake was self-consciously watching and waiting, and when McMurtry finally gave him the book back, he moved, as quickly as possible without seeming too eager, into the kitchen to read the inscription, which he felt certain, all things considered, was bound to be special and personal. "After all," Shrake said, "I had known McMurtry in Austin when he came through there and stayed with Billie Lee." So he opened the book and read what it said: "Best Wishes, Larry McMurtry."

Old man Dobie was still around in 1962, like a figure from Olympus. He could cause members of the state legislature (many formerly his students at UT) to blush with shame for a moment before rushing back to do their dirty work. I knew several people who actually heard, in person, Dobie's famous "shit detector" speech to the House of Representatives when that distinguished group was on the verge of passing some obscene, racially-motivated legislation. It was exciting to live in a place where a writer and teacher could get a rise out of a politician. Bob Eckhardt, Don Kennard, Babe Schwartz, Malcolm McGregor, John Hannah, John Henry Faulk, Maury Maverick, Jr., H. G. Wells (the one from Tulia), Bill Kugle, Franklin Spears, Larry Goodwyn, Warren Burnet and others fought the good fight against the Philistines. They lost most of the time, of course—the Philistines were in the majority. But they won a skirmish here and a point there, anyway, which was better than nothing.

This was back when Texas Republicans were ashamed to admit to belonging to that party. So, we had what was ostensibly a one-party state, except during presidential elections, when it reverted briefly to a two-party state. There were Democrats for Eisenhower, and so on, but for statewide, county and city races, we had only one party—Democrats. They were, however, divided into two major divisions: Conservatives (which included mostly Republicans in Democrats' clothing) and Moderate-to-Liberals, who more or less went along with the thrust of the national party. There were also, among the electorate, so-called Brass Collar Democrats, those Texans who voted Democrat because of a vestige of resentment left over from the Great Depression and the Civil War (Civil War resentment being handed down from one generation to the next). At that particular time, John Connally was front man for the secret Republican wing, and Ralph Yarborough was spiritual leader of the populist-liberal-brass collar wing. In some ways, that system was easier to understand than the criss-crossing loyalties and influences in the two-party epoch of the 1980s and 1990s.

But it was the next decade, the 1970s, when McMurtry and other Maddogs blossomed into stars that shone beyond the borders of the Lone Star State.

We've become a people who want nearly everything in packages, neat and convenient, even the years gone by. Packaging history in decades is all right, I suppose. At least it breaks things down into chunks small enough to examine and maybe make up fantasies about what it all meant. The seventies were a hard act to follow. The sixties were mostly up front, picketing and declaring and demanding. That decade actually began about 1964 and didn't really wind down until about 1974. There was some excitement stirred up here and there in the seventies, but for the most part, it was a laid-back decade. Laid back and waiting, it seemed to me.

Let me say now that I don't intend to get into the obvious and deadly serious stuff here—the Mideast crises, the China Syndrome syndrome, the gasoline price spirals, the semi-impeachment of Richard Nixon, the end of that crazy old Asian war, inflation, the space development following the moon shot in 1969. I leave such as that to the depth bomb crews and chronic worriers. Somebody has do it, but not me, right now. I was an editorial writer for years and nobody paid any attention that I could tell.

My conclusion about the seventies, when the 1980s threatened to come down on us, was this: a decade that gave us Willie Nelson and Earl Campbell couldn't be all bad. It was in the 1970s that Willie and Waylon and Jerry Jeff and a handful of Texas prose writers managed to create Texas chic even on the isle of Manhattan. And it could get downright crazy in Austin and Dallas and Fort Worth and Luchenbach and, sometimes, Houston and other spots around the state.

McMurtry had kind of exploded upon the literary scene, in his home state and elsewhere, as the seventies opened with the release of the movie made from his novel, *The Last Picture Show*.

I was teaching journalism at SMU then and escorted a small group of my students to Washington, D. C. and New York City during the holidays between the fall and spring semesters. The D. C. stopover featured a night of conversation with Larry L. King, and the next evening's visit was with McMurtry at his home. I had given the students a list of books and magazine articles to read in preparation for the trip. They would be meeting Willie Morris and David Halberstam in New York City. They had been reading the Willie Morris-edited editions of *Harper's* and were duly impressed by the work of King, Morris and Halberstam. But Larry McMurtry was not yet a name that lit up their eyes. King had fascinated them and kept them up most of the night before, so when we taxied into northwest Washington to McMurtry's home, they were weary and ready to get this assignment over with as soon as possible.

According to my friend Joe Murray, 1970 was almost thirty years ago. That may explain why I don't remember all the specifics about that session in McMurtry's living room, except that it was cozy and chatty, and the students left more awake than when they arrived. But the excitement burst forth concerning McMurtry only after we had returned to Dallas and were into the spring semester. It was then that the movie, *The Last Picture Show*, opened in Big D. For days after that opening, students who had been sleepily impressed by the Texas author's friendliness and willingness to answer all their questions—both the intelligent and the stupid—ran into my office, in pairs and trios and singles, all atwitter, sputtering "You mean, that's the same Larry McMurtry we spent an evening with in Washington?"

● ● ●

During the visit my students and I enjoyed with McMurtry at his home in Washington, D. C., Larry and I wandered together into his kitchen, to refill some chip bowls or something, and he said to me, "I apologize for stealing your hearse." As luck would have it, I had not read Larry's latest (at that time) novel *Moving On*, and didn't know what he was talking about. Somehow, however, I sensed he was referring to something in that novel. So, being a straight-forward, honest young man from Lubbock, I said, "Ahh, that's okay." Then Larry said something to the effect that Billie Lee Brammer had told him about my hearse, and it had fit perfectly with a character in *Moving On*, so he stuck it in there. At last, I could tell him the truth. "Don't apologize," I said. "I'm flattered." And I was, and am. At the first opportunity, of course, I grabbed a copy of *Moving On* and read it.

Sure enough, in Chapter Two, Sonny Shanks, the dashing, handsome, and somewhat rascally rodeo champion, owns a hearse. To quote from page 36:

> For years Shanks had driven Cadillac hearses—
> they were an essential part of his legend. The
> hearses were white and he always had three sets
> of bulls' horns painted in gold on each one: A
> set on each door and one on the top, so people
> in airplanes would know it was him, he said.

My hearse wasn't white, it was classic black with that buffalo hump over the cab. I had no longhorns painted on it anywhere, but it was a hearse, and I had been traveling about Texas in it in those pre-suburban van times. I naturally dubbed my hearse "William Randolph." We shared some fun adventures, including an unexpected overnight stay in Fort Stockton, a town on the long lonely highway between Austin and El Paso, down near the Mexican border and the Big Bend. I was working for Willie Morris's weekly version of *The Texas Observer* then. John Connally had just been elected governor. Willie sent me to El Paso to confer with Malcolm McGregor and others for a follow-up story on the election.

It was just getting dark when a highway patrolman stopped me somewhere between Austin and Junction after clocking us at what he said was eighty miles per hour. I had been distracted by counting deer along the roadside and had gotten up to thirty-seven when I noticed the flashing lights behind me and pulled over. The state trooper was exceedingly nice. He examined the back end of my hearse, saw the bedding and trunk, and said, admiringly, "Man, I bet this is a great hunting and fishing vehicle." I allowed as how he was sure right about that, although I had been hunting only once and that was years before I owned the hearse, and I'd captured a total of three fish in my life. There weren't a whole bunch of handy places to fish on the panhandle when I was growing up out there. (I notice they have lakes up there now.) Anyhow, since we had bonded, the state trooper let me go with a verbal warning. He said he'd been on the lookout for speeding teenagers on that long strip of straight highway. They tended to use it for drag racing at times, he said. I thanked him from the bottom of my heart and continued on toward faraway El Paso.

I made a point of staying within the speed limit from there on, but as I was skimming along the flat, straight highway somewhere in the wide open spaces before you get to Fort Stockton, I began noticing what I thought was the motor cutting off briefly and then picking up again. I was very aware of every knock and tick because, after all, William Randolph was no young kid. Soon, I spotted an isolated gas station at a cross road ahead and pulled in there. The man came bounding out to meet me, dragging a water hose. I said, "When you get me filled up with supreme, how about checking out the motor— I think it's cutting out on me now and then." He grinned and said he'd do that as soon as he put out the fire on my wheel.

I'd wondered about the water hose, but figured he was going to check my water too. People who ran gas stations did such as that back then. I jumped out and, sure enough, William Randolph's left rear tire was flaming brightly in the desert twilight. After putting the fire out, the man jacked it up, looked the situation over, and concluded the brakes were worn down to the nub and the friction, which had been causing that sensation of the motor cutting out briefly on me back there, had eventually sparked the fire. The fire, in turn, had warped the rear axle. I was told this after being towed into Fort Stockton. The mechanic there told me also that he would have to order a new axle from Odessa and it wouldn't get there until some-time the next day.

So, I spent rest of the night in Fort Stockton, and much of the next day. I found myself wondering what a real Maddog would do if he got himself stranded in Fort Stockton over-night, and decided he would find a bar somewhere and have a drink with the locals. I walked downstairs from my hotel room and out into the downtown Fort Stockton night. A few blocks from the hotel I found a likely spot, a bar with no win-dows in front and a litter of pickup trucks along the western wall of the cement block building. When I opened the front door a gust of Mexican music, along with the clacking of pool balls, the shuffling of booted feet, and chitchat in Spanish washed over me. By the time I had taken two steps in from the sidewalk, all sounds had ceased except the music, and all eyes had turned toward my entrance. It struck me suddenly that I was the only Anglo in the place.

I struggled with the fear that rose in my chest, telling myself I was reacting like an ignorant bigot—reacting to ste-reotypes left over from childhood. I strolled with deliberate nonchalance to the bar and ordered a shot of tequila and drank it down in one long swallow without looking right or left. Then I dropped a five dollar bill on the bar, turned abruptly and walked back outside. The tequila burned my stomach as I hurried back to the hotel and up to my room, undressed and climbed into the creaking bed.

I lay there, my hands behind my head, staring at the ceil-ing, thinking: You can take the boy out of West Texas, but it is not easy to erase West Texas from the boy, even if he's been all the way to New York City and back.

Larry L. King, The Writer from Texas, Not the Guy on TV

Very late one night in the latter 1960s, a loud knock on the front door of my home near the TCU campus in Fort Worth woke me from a deep sleep. A second and third bam from the front of the house got me out of bed and I stumbled to the door, opened it (a stupid move, since I hadn't checked to see who was there) and a brawny, heavy shouldered body burst by me, followed by two young children. The room was still dark, but I could see the burly body's outstretched arms and hear their owner declare in a familiar authoritative bass voice: "Spread out, kids, and find a place to lay down. This is where we shall spend the night."

As I had almost immediately recognized, even in the dark, the interloper was Larry L. King—not the scrawny-shouldered, suspendered fellow on CNN, but the one my mother called "your Larry King"—who at the time was one of the nation's best and most prolific freelance magazine writers, and who later would become the only Texas Tech dropout to attend Harvard, teach at Princeton, write a bunch of books and co-author a Broadway hit musical, *The Best Little Whorehouse in Texas*.

My Larry King was living in Washington, D. C., at the time. Moved up there from Midland where he'd starred, somewhat, on the high school football team, worked as a reporter for the local daily and interviewed prominent citizens and an occasional itinerant celebrity on the local radio station. King had pulled up his West Texas roots in 1954 to work in the nation's capital for the then newly-elected West Texas congressman, J. T. (Slick) Rutherford, who liked to call himself the "Cowboy Statesman." After the Cowboy Statesman fell upon bad times, King went to work in the offices of Texas congressman Jim Wright and toiled there until 1964, when he decided to hurl caution into the storm and do what he'd always wanted to do—devote his energies and mind to making his living as a writer, exclusively. He had a novel almost finished and had sold a couple of magazine pieces, so the time seemed ripe to make the Big Move.

We met that same year in the District of Columbia, where I had gone to surrender, as mentioned previously. We were introduced by a mutual friend, Ralph Hutto, a buddy of mine back in Mississippi when we worked on competing newspapers covering the same beat: city hall, in Jackson. Hutto had moved to Washington to work for the Senate Judicial Committee—a move that brought him a great deal more money than he had been making as a beat reporter—along with a weighty measure of guilt he tried, unsuccessfully, to hide from me, since we had been fervent liberals together in Mississippi during its most dangerous era (to liberals and people of color), the days just before and right after the Supreme Court's 1954 desegregation decision. But that's another story.

"I know this fellow from Texas name of Larry King you ought to meet," Hutto told me, and arranged for us to get together at a favorite Capitol Hill watering hole in the basement of the old Plaza Hotel. King and I soon found that we

knew many of the same people back in Texas and we had our
West Texas tall tales to tell; so, we jabbered and laughed and
entertained each other until, after a spell, we looked up to
find that our friend Hutto had left. Lawrence and I have remained friends ever since.

Almost thirty-five years later, Cox Newspaper columnist
Joe Murray and I sipped Diet Cokes in the living room of
King's sumptuous Washington home near Rock Creek Park,
where he lived with his wife Barbara (who was younger than
my oldest daughter) and their son and daughter, both younger
than my grandchildren, and talked with him about his early
days in Washington.

His first trip to the District was by train, King remembered. "It was morning and suddenly I see all these cars feed-
ing off the road onto the one highway, and I'm thinking, 'All
them sum-bitches are going the same direction. I wonder if
there's some sort of atom bomb threat!'" It turned out to be
nothing more than the regular morning rush hour traffic,
which was a bit heavier than what he'd seen in Midland. Soon
King was accustomed to the steady stream of traffic and became part of it.

But when King first arrived in the nation's capital back in
1954, he had some difficulty finding a place to live. "I'd see an
ad in the paper and call about it and they'd tell me the apartment had been rented already and hang up," he recalled, shaking his massive head with the New England sea captain's chin
whiskers he'd worn for many years. "Finally, a friend of mine
suggested the property managers might be thinking I was
colored because of my West Texas accent." Sure enough, once
he followed up the ads in person, King discovered he could
have his pick of any apartment he could afford. That was
then. "Capitol Hill at that time," King remembered, "had five

thousand people or less working there. Now, I understand it's got thirty-nine thousand employees, or more."

Even after deciding to become a full-time writer, King stayed in Washington, although he could have lived almost anywhere. "Originally, I had a wife from Texas—actually from Oklahoma—and she never liked it here. We split up in 1963 after thirteen years. Wasn't long after that I quit Congress to be a sink-or-swim, full-time writer. By then, I had fallen in love with a young woman who was a native of D. C. and wanted to stay here. We got married and stayed until she died in 1972, very young, of cancer. Then I wanted to get out of this town. It held a lot of bad memories for me. So I moved off to New York and was very happy there.

"I used to have these fantasies about retiring down to Texas," King went on, "about how I'd go back and get me a ranch about forty miles out of Austin. I'd sit there under a majestic oak tree and receive statesmen and scholars and people who wanted to know the secret of life, and I'd tell them. The Sons of the Pioneers would be providing the background music. It'd be bucolic and wonderful and I could drive into Austin in half an hour.

"But my present wife, Barbara, who was from Corpus Christi originally and was up here working in a Washington law firm, had been East to college and had lost all desire to live in Texas. 'Look,' she said, 'you can move a typewriter anywhere, and I can't move a law practice.' But it's very nice and comfortable. John D. Rockefeller couldn't have a house and grounds in New York City like we have here because there ain't none there."

This was after *The Best Little Whorehouse in Texas* had placed King in the category we in West Texas used to call "well fixed." So, these days, King is a famous Texas expatriate who, according to Joe Murray, after thirty-six years now has a thicker Texas accent than many who never lived anywhere but the Lone Star State.

The Texas accent-endurance phenomenon may have something to do with other things than simply growing up on a farm or in a family with one foot still on the farm or ranch out there in West Texas—or Central Texas, or East or South Texas. I've pondered the possibility that it could have something to do with the West Texas altitude (more than 3,000 feet above sea level, and flat as a pancake) or the climate (there are seasons, but few visible symbols of seasonal change. The ever-present wind gets colder or warmer—no big deal about autumnal color changes and all that). Or maybe it's the distant horizon that distinguishes West Texans and makes them recognizable to each other as they mix and mingle, wherever they may be. (We do have sort of squinty eyes.)

Once at a party in Greenwich Village when I was living in New York, a lady stood listening in on a conversation I was participating in and, after awhile, she said, "You're from the Texas or Oklahoma panhandle country, aren't you?" I admitted I was, but didn't tell her I had lived in Mississippi more than a decade after leaving Texas and just prior to moving to Manhattan three years earlier. It's my theory that most other accents would have disappeared or altered considerably over that length of time, but my Texas twang, like King's, seemed to have thickened.

The unmistakable mien and manner of West Texan males has as much to do with physical appearance as drawling speech. I can't put my finger on it, but there's a West Texas look. Waylon Jennings has it. So did Buddy Holly, who didn't look anything like Waylon, except for a certain indefinable something that is West Texan. Country rocker Joe Ely is from Lubbock, and I knew it the first time I looked at him up close.

When I met Lee Clayton, the picker poet who wrote a number of songs recorded by Waylon and Willie, I recognized his Lubbockness immediately. I knew he had to be a Lubbock boy, or at least from somewhere in that vicinity, on the high plains.

But I digress . . .

Back in the late sixties when King was stopping by my house in Fort Worth on a semi-regular basis, he was primarily a magazine writer—writing mostly for the Willie Morris-edited *Harper's*, and occasionally for *Life*, *Playboy* and *Esquire*. He would come through Cowtown on his way to and from assignments and/or visits with his children who lived in Midland with their mother. Sometimes I would arrange bull sessions with King and a group of journalism students, sessions enjoyed as thoroughly by King as by the students. Lawrence was quite a natural raconteur. I served as straight man (having already heard most of his stories) in King's sit-down comedy-history-philosophy performances.

Sometimes, King's visits were simply an opportunity for us both to relax from our daily grind and indulge ourselves in our separate, widely ranging imaginations. There was one memorable evening we co-authored "An Ode to George Jones." That piece, the original handwritten composition, now rests for the benefit of posterity in the special archives of the Southwest Texas State University Library Southwestern Writers Collection in San Marcos, among the works of Texas writers, their letters and memorabilia.

I discovered to my considerable chagrin that not only did my friend Lawrence not remember the George Jones poem, he didn't even remember the night of our collaboration. But he called Dick Holland, who was the Writers Collection curator then. Dick punched it up on their library computer and mailed it to me for inclusion in this important memoir.

This isn't all of it, but it should give you the general idea:

ODE TO GEORGE JONES

Whether you is away
or at your home
Everybody loves to hear George Jones.

North or south or east or west
He's the one we love the best.

Look there, under the chair
And lookee over there
George Jones is ever where.

Roses are red
Violets are large
Ever body loves Jones comma George.

And so on and on, into the night. And, I must remind you, this was in the late sixties, long before George Jones was cool. You could say King and I were on the cutting edge—as true poets usually are.

Not all of King's time away from his beloved ancient Olivetti was devoted to fun and games and poetry composition. He spent time and money supporting the artistic efforts of needy Fellow Texans—Billie Lee Brammer in particular. As other Maddogs did from time to time, King made a sincere effort to "save" Billie Lee from himself. This was not easily done. Both Bud Shrake and Dan Jenkins, for instance, had contributed efforts and even money to the Brammer project, to no noticeable avail. Once Shrake and Jenkins finagled a *Sports Illustrated* editor into assigning a story to Brammer with

an advance for expenses to travel to the Left Coast to interview a boxer of renown at the time. After several weeks, there
was no word from Brammer back at *SI* headquarters and the
editor who had given him the assignment wired his last known
address asking for a progress report. Billie Lee wired back
that the project was going well, but would take more time
and, therefore more expense money. More money was wired
his way forthwith, and Billie Lee apparently disappeared from
the face of the earth, never to be heard from again until Shrake
accidentally ran into him months later on the street in Austin.

"I didn't even ask him about the story," Shrake sighed.

As to King's attempt to help save Billie Lee, and incidentally help himself at the same time, Brammer knew King had
signed a contract to do a book about Lyndon Baines Johnson.
Brammer, you will remember, had earlier received a sizable
advance from some out-of-touch publisher to do a book about
the former president and fellow Texan. One day in Austin,
King ran into Brammer, who offered to sell Lawrence the "ex-
tensive" research notes, quotes and so on he had accumu-
lated over the years during and after he had worked for LBJ.

"I'm never going to write that book," Brammer admitted
truthfully, "so you may as well benefit from my years of research. I'll sell it to you for a thousand dollars."

"I had known Billie Lee a long time by then," King told me
years later, "so I wasn't about to let him hornswoggle me again
and I drove a hard bargain. I told him I'd give him five hundred now and five hundred when he delivered the goods."

"Well, I went home and waited and waited and nothing
arrived in the mail, so I called Brammer and chewed his ass
out. He was astonished that I hadn't received his years' worth
of notes and interviews and told me he would call this former
girlfriend of his in New Orleans where it was all stored and

have her send it immediately. Finally, one day the UPS man rang my doorbell in Washington and delivered this large box postmarked Austin. I was really excited and tore it open and found it filled with old issues of *Time* and *Newsweek*. Nothing else.

"I was furious," King went on. "I could have looked up everything in those magazines in the library. I called Billie Lee and chewed him out again. He was once again astonished, of course, and said he didn't know what that woman in New Orleans could have been thinking about. I said, 'Billie Lee, the box was postmarked Austin, not New Orleans.' He sputtered and I hung up, vowing never again to fall for one of his scams. And I didn't—for at least six months."

Before King made his fortune on *The Best Little Whorehouse in Texas*, Willie Morris maneuvered him a Nieman fellowship at Harvard. It was Morris's belief that, if King had time and direction to study and think deep thoughts, he could become considerably more than simply a damn good magazine writer. So, King went to Harvard during the school year of 1969 and 1970. As luck would have it, my former boss at the *New York Herald Tribune*, Dwight Sargent was, at that time, curator of the Nieman Foundation's Harvard program for journalists.

King and Sargent, early in the school year, got together and came up with the idea of appointing me "Journalist in Residence," so I could spend time at the Cambridge institution's journalism study and discussion program along with a crew of outstanding newspaper and magazine writers and editors from around the country. That year's Nieman fellows were a classy group. I remember Headrick Smith, then of the *New York Times*, and Gene Goltz, winner of not one but two Pulitzers for his work at the *Detroit Free Press*; Wallace Terry of *Time* magazine, and there were others probably even more prominent in their respective fields that I have since forgotten. I was there only two weeks and was unable to get acquainted with all of them. But it was a memorable experience.

I stayed at the Harvard Faculty Club, with its leather chairs and historical ambiance as thick as Houston humidity. There was one afternoon Harvard students rioted on the streets around the square, breaking out the windows of several local business establishments. That evening, on local news broadcasts, the president of one of the Cambridge banks whose windows had been smashed came on and declared that until the United States straightened out its bungling and senseless ways in Vietnam, such things were bound to happen. I tried to imagine a similar statement coming from a Texas banker under those circumstances, but I couldn't manage it. And I have a rather active imagination if I do say so.

As Fate, or whomsoever gods are in charge of that sort of thing, would have it, by the time I arrived on the scene in Cambridge, my two advocates—King and Sargent—were no longer chums but on opposite sides of a tussle that had developed between Sargent and some Nieman fellows regarding, near as I could tell, the selection of speakers for the sessions attended by the fellows and invited guests from the Harvard faculty and the local daily, the *Boston Globe*. I'm not certain King was himself a leader of the revolt, but he was enthusiastically right in the big middle.

To the credit of both sides, the revolution apparently was carried on, by both sides, in a gentlemanly manner which would not have upset even the most conservative alumni of that great university. Well, maybe the *most* conservative alums would have been upset, but certainly not middle of the road graduates and most certainly not those who had graduated only recently into and out of the hectic times that were the sixties and early seventies.

Anyhow, by the time I arrived, my two patrons were barely speaking to each other and there were two separate sessions being conducted. The "underground" (as it was sometimes called in the vernacular of the times) selected one set of speakers and curator Sargent and his faction picked the official speakers. The Nieman Foundation paid for both programs and everybody, with the exception of Sargent, attended both sessions. At least that's how I remember it. Being a guest of the program, I attended both sessions—the underground gatherings with King and the official ones with Sargent, which puzzled some of the Fellows. "What are you doing here anyhow?" Headrick Smith asked me at a farewell party given by Wally Terry and King for me the night before I caught the plane back to Texas. He told me there was a rumor going around that I was slated to replace Sargent as curator, among other things, but no one could figure out for sure why I was present at both sessions and seemed to sit beside Sargent at the official sessions and with King at the underground sessions.

On April 7, 1970, about the middle of my Harvard stay, I wrote a long letter to some of my pet journalism pupils back at Southern Methodist University. Quoting from that letter might help set the true tone of my Nieman experience better than my sketchy memory at this distance. For instance, the following segment should be quoted to balance what I may have inferred in previous paragraphs: "Anyhow, the rebels have their private sessions and I am invited. And Sargent invites me places with him. So, you can see I am often on the horns of that famous beast with two of them. Sargent, however, is more reasonable than most of these ornery but lovable Nieman fellers think he is; so, I've had no embarrassing moments yet . . . "

Then there is a part where I comment, out of my 1960s frame of mind, about one of the prominent speakers, Hedley Donovan, then editor-in-chief at Time-Life, Inc.: "These Nieman Fellows—like so many good reporters—are not timid a bit. They listened politely to Hedley Donovan's brief talk, then went at him hot and heavy. I must report—and I do so reluctantly—that this session left me with a heavy heart— that the boss of one of the largest news and publishing organizations in the world doesn't know his ass about the First Amendment."

● ● ●

When King moved to New York City after his wife Rosemary died, he was widely known in the magazine business but less in show business celebrity circles than he would become later after the success of *The Best Little Whorehouse in Texas*. But Lawrence's Texas friends, Shrake and Jenkins, had been living and working in Manhattan for some time by then and they knew all the "In" places, like Elaine's and P. J. Clarke's. So, they showed King around. One night in P. J. Clarke's famous back room where only the famous and privileged and their guests were allowed to sip and sup, King was sipping with Shrake when Lauren Bacall walked in alone and sat at a table near them.

"Good Gawd!" King stage-whispered, "that's Lauren Bacall! She's my favorite actress. I'd give anything to meet her."

"Well, go over and introduce yourself," Shrake urged. "It'll probably please her. You know how these show business people are."

"Really? You think that'd be all right?"

"Sure," encouraged Shrake. "Give her a thrill."

So King got to his feet and lumbered over to the famous actress's table. "Miz Bacall," he said. "You don't know me, but you've been my favorite . . ."

About there was where Miz Bacall interrupted our hero with a frown and, in her famous sexy voice, growled these immortal words: "Fuck off, Buster."

King, studied his feet, shook his head and muttered, "Damn that Shrake. He's done it to me again."

When Rosemary King was in the hospital being treated for the cancer that would kill her, I spent a week with Larry in their D.C. apartment. He had called that he needed company. Said he was going mad worrying about her and if, when she died, his writing would dry up.

"It all started with her and it might stop when she goes," he worried.

When I arrived, I found King had been staying up all night, not at his typewriter as he had from time to time in the past, but on the long distance telephone, giving friends and enemies hell for vague reasons, and drinking, of course. He was, indeed, going mad. But he seemed to calm down some when I'd been there a day or two. Oh, he raved at me for wearing his new leather jacket he'd urged me to wear in the first place and he raged at me for folding before midnight and for one or two other eccentric things I did all the time and had always done without thinking. But generally speaking, King calmed down some.

One evening we went to hear Mickey Newberry, the ultra-talented Texas singer/songwriter who was performing at a club in town. Larry had met Newberry in Nashville where he was researching a piece for *Harpers* on something having to do with country music and musicians. He'd kind of featured Newberry in the article and Newberry, who was just rising as a performer at that time, had gratefully invited King to come by the hotel where he and his new wife were staying while he was doing a week at the D. C. night club.

During our taxi ride to the hotel where the Newberrys were staying, King and I rehearsed ways to trick him into picking and singing for us in his hotel room. Just for us, in a private concert. We laughed a lot about it and allowed as how none of our schemes would ever work; after all, the man was a professional! And, as King pointed out, asking him to sing for us would be like somebody asking us to write for them while they watched.

But when we arrived at the hotel and were invited into their room by the lovely Mrs. Newberry, we heard Mickey yelling, "Come on in here and listen to this." And he sang a new song he had written. He continued to play and sing for us until it was time for us to go to the club for his gig. That was the first time it registered with me that most musicians would be doing what they do whether they got paid for it or not. Just because they love the way it makes them feel.

That evening at the club, yet another special kick to King's ego was bestowed when the pretty and talented young female songwriter/singer who opened for Newberry announced that in the audience was a young writer named Larry King who had inspired her to become a songwriter when she read his novel, *The One-Eyed Man*.

The next night, King and I decided to take Larry McMurtry, who also lived in D. C. in those days and, besides writing his books, helped run a rare book store he co-owned. When Newberry's opening singer took the stage that night, she announced that in the audience was a young man who was very special to her named Larry McMurtry, who was the author of a book that had inspired her to become a songwriter. I think she named *The Last Picture Show* as her inspiration.

Willie Morris came down from New York a couple of nights later and we took him to hear Newberry too, although King was at first hesitant to do so because, he said, "He'll talk while Mickey's singing." And he did. But the most amazing thing was that the young woman opened her show that night by announcing—I swear it's true—that in the audience that evening was a young writer whose book, *North Toward Home*, had inspired her to become a songwriter, and his name was Willie Morris.

I confess I was a little hurt and probably would have given her a copy of my own novel, *Incident at Ashton*, for inspiration if I'd had a copy.

A vital part of King's achievement as a writer, as well as his success as a friend and orator, has to do with his incredible energy and drive. He has gone through periods when he wrote long letters to me every few weeks, and I know I wasn't the only friend he was corresponding with. His letters are almost as entertaining as his essays and plays. I donated most of mine, with King's permission (at his insistence, as a matter of fact) to the Southwestern Writers Collection. But now and again I run across one of his letters stuck somewhere deep inside my files, as I did recently. This one not only passes along personal information and salutations, but gives the reader an idea of the pace and scope of King's work, even though he is now into his sixties (his early sixties, mind you). Many people refer to this age as the ordinary person's slowing down period—their Golden Years. But nobody ever accused Larry L. King, the West Texas whirlwind, of being "ordinary."

Anyhow, here's the letter, just as he wrote it, dated March 16, 1990:

Dear Onkle Jake:

Here's you a batch of West Texas culture: the final Demo Tape of them C&W songs I sold to that gullible music publishing house. Son Brad's doing vocals and lead guitar and one of the arrangements. Guess the songs ain't too bad for a fellow who don't read, sing or play a note of music. Meaning myownself. Publisher soon starts sending tape around to sangers, their management types and agents. Don't know if anything will happen, but I've had fun and obviously, advanced the Cultural Standards of the Western World by about 27 degrees. (I dubbed this tape on a new-fangled double-deck tape machine Brad got me for Christmas; seems to me it records upside down and backwards, so I may have put the label on the wrong side of the cassett. Just keep turning it and fiddling with it until you hear music, in case I messed up.)

Me'n Lawyer Blaine [his wife Barbara] spent fifteen days in Paris, Florence, Venice and London recently. I actually dreaded most of it, but dam if I didn't have a great time. Lawyer Blaine had so much fun she actually hugged my neck naked several times. Venice sure is different. Especially from Putnam and Odessa.

Went to N.Y. earlier in week for story conference to shape second draft of Hank Williams moom [sic] picture. That director lady, Joan Micklin Silver, sure seems to know what she's doing. I'm to have first 1/3 of second draft—forty to forty-five pages—on her desk by April 4th, and it's zipping along purty good.

Got to quit and go to school conference with Lindsay's [his daughter's] teachers, so they can tell me she's the most brilliant girl in the history of the 4th grade. Them teachers is slick.

Lemme know what you think of these wonderful Christian ballads.

All best, ol' friend, from

Larry L. King.

For those interested in the ups and downs of the process of writing a successful Broadway musical, I enthusiastically recommend you read King's book, *The Whorehouse Papers*. It reads like a good novel and pretty much brings you up to snuff on King's transition from a successful, but almost broke, magazine freelancer to successful and rich co-author of a hit Broadway musical. It's one helluva tale, filled not only with philosophical and psychological suspense, foppery and courage, but romance and everything else a good novel needs. And it's fact, not fiction.

The stress of two years of concentrated work on *The Best Little Whorehouse in Texas*—during which time he wrote almost nothing else and was, therefore, nearing bankruptcy by opening night—added to King's natural inclination toward the use of strong drink and chemicals known to alter one's mental state. Followed by the shock of sudden gigantic success, this caused our hero to tiptoe to the brink of mental and physical disaster.

We had not been in close touch during the period King was working on *Whorehouse* and the time immediately following its tremendous success. Then, something came up that caused me to write him a letter, which King didn't answer for so long I had forgotten writing it in the first place. Finally, one day I received a letter from him that began something like this: "Dear Onkle Jake, Barbara pushed your letter through the bars . . ." And he went on to explain that apparently he had flipped out and had been running around in Austin chasing old ladies with meat cleavers, or some such ridiculous conduct, and his young lawyer wife had caused him to be committed to one of those places where they force you to save your own life by drying out and getting your ducks back in a row. I can't recall exactly what year that was, but it was sometime in the early 1980s, and as far as I know (and I have my sources), my friend Lawrence has been stone sober ever since. He swears by AA and once at lunch with him in D. C., I listened while King and our waiter got into a warm discussion about the last AA meeting they had attended.

One of my D. C. sources has been former East Texas Congressman Good Time Charlie Wilson of Lufkin, who was an old drinking and hanging out buddy of King's during his wet years and who has complained that lately King isn't near as much fun since he quit drinking. This seems to be the case for a number of Maddogs. They may not be as jolly as they once were to former drinking buddies, but they are still alive.

Gary Cartwright
and June Allyson

I remember a pithy exchange between me and Gary Cartwright not long after I met in him in 1961. It was a brief conversational gem that should have tipped me off to Cartwright's basic genius for telling a long and complex story with a few, well-chosen words. This was back before it became widely known that Gary was a world-class reporter whose work was much too expansive for the confines of a daily newspaper column. In 1961 he was still learning his craft, but the essence of his greatness (no, that's not an exaggeration; that's reporting: the man is great at what he does) as a witness who not only discerns the truth but is able to tell you what he saw and heard in a manner that's not hard to follow, even in the most complex situations, was evident.

Anyhow, back in 1961, during the week or two since I had last seen Gary, he and his wife Barbara had, as we said in those days, "separated." He moved out of their North Dallas home into an apartment just off North Central Expressway not far from SMU with Bud Shrake, his old running buddy from as far back as their sportswriting days at the late, lamented *Fort Worth Press*. Coincidentally, or not, Shrake had recently separated from his first wife, Joyce.

"What happened, Gary?" I asked—rather stupidly, I realized as soon as the words were out of my mouth and suspended in the air between us.

"She threw my incense burner out in the back yard," Cartwright said seriously.

I laughed, and those I told what he'd said laughed. The incense burner anecdote became one of the favorite "Jap stories" there for awhile—told around campfires in Austin and Dallas, until other, better Jap stories shoved it too far to the end of the line to be noticed any longer.

One of the latest Cartwright stories, of course, is the one about his labeling Deion Sanders, the Dallas Cowboys star, as a go-straight-home-after-work family man, unlike some of his more frivolous teammates. This observation appeared in a *Texas Monthly* feature, which came out almost simultaneously with the news that Neon Deion's wife was suing him for divorce and blaming the breakup on adultery. Cartwright admitted to questions by the press that he had been fooled by Sanders and further acknowledged it wasn't the first time his judgment had failed him as a reporter and pundit. Way back in his sportswriting days, he said, he'd predicted that a young athlete who'd played quarterback for TCU and was seven or eight feet tall would be a big time star as a pro. Unfortunately, the ex-Frog quarterback lasted only one or two plays in a Dallas Cowboys exhibition game and was never heard from again in the football world.

But after the Sanders divorce proceedings came to an amicable and almost immediate halt and Deion announced that he was now a born-again Christian, I remembered that Shrake once told me he had thought about it and thought about it over the years and had come to the conclusion that everything Cartwright said eventually turned out to be true. After mulling this over, we agreed that it was, indeed, frightening to contemplate. I could just picture a very tall, white-haired, bent ex-TCU quarterback making a heralded hall of fame comeback in place of the wounded Troy Aikman.

I had already come to realize some time before Shrake's pronouncement that Jap's seemingly casual punchline reply to my unconsciously broad query, "What happened?" actually answered my questions completely. It was all there. You just had to use your imagination to picture all of the drama, and melodrama, and real pain and comedy that led to Barbara Cartwright's finally, ultimately, grabbing the damn incense burner and tossing it, angrily, out the door and into the back yard.

Not long before the legendary incense burner episode, Barbara had asked me: "Tell me, Jay, how do you live with a writer?" I think I told Barbara she was asking the wrong person. If I didn't, I should have—because, by that time, I had been divorced twice myself, to my considerable shame and embarrassment, both psychologically and financially. It was only a few years, however, until my sorry marital status became far from uncommon. Not that it made me feel any better about that part of my life. But company does at least, partially, reduce the misery of shame.

I saw June Allyson on television the other night, hawking those diapers for old-timers, and it occurred to me that it was her fault so many men and women of my generation had wound up D-I-V-O-R-C-E-D. The generation that came before mine was convinced, for various reasons, that divorce was not the answer. One major reason for that, probably, was that in those bygone days, only a few women with special talents and insights and extraordinary opportunities—or trust funds—

could make it in the man's world outside the home and hearth. Not that the circumstances have turned all the way around yet, but some things for women have changed somewhat since then and seem to be headed in the right direction.

Anyhow, my own peer group, I'm afraid, ventured first into the alien terrain of divorce in sizable numbers and started the dysfunctional family ball rolling, so to speak. The institution of marriage hasn't been the same since the 1950s, and probably never will be again. And it's all June Allyson's fault. That's my theory, and I'm sticking to it. If you are too young to remember all of those June Allyson movies from the forties and fifties, or if you've missed the reruns on television in more recent times, I'll explain.

June Allyson was the one with the cute little button nose and that innocent-but sexy voice and cheerleader's body who endured so much so prettily for the love of all those dashing leading men. Regardless of how bad the trouble was, how thoughtlessly her man behaved, June always endured courageously and cried only when her man was not around to see and hear. And her love never wavered, regardless of how wrongheaded old Jimmy Stewart ("young" Jimmy Stewart I should say), Dick Powell and Gary Cooper and others always managed to get themselves into sticky situations—in war and peace—but plucky, reliable, true-blue June never complained or took her love to town. She certainly never nagged. She never even mussed her jaunty blond pageboy hairdo and perfect makeup—much less raised her delectable voice in anger.

Bette Davis, on the other hand, tried her darndest to show us how the world really was—to warn us—by portraying women who were so mean and bitchy that anyone who wasn't hopelessly in love with June Allyson would have suspected there were women out there who would cut off your nose to spite your face, so to speak, if you so much as looked sideways. Bette tried to alert us there were lots of women out there who wouldn't stand for any of that crap little June put up with so gallantly and prettily.

But did we pay any attention to old Bette's message? Noooo.

So, around half of all marriages from the sixties on seem to be doomed to fall apart somewhere down the line . . . When she finally tosses his incense burner out the back door.

Don't get me wrong. I believe in the institution of marriage. I believe in it very much. Otherwise, I wouldn't have tried it so many times. But it is true that long term, happy marriages have become the exception rather than the rule. I remember how surprised I was when my daughter Carter was in junior high and came home one day and told me she was the only kid she knew who lived with her father. All the rest lived with their mothers, she said. I was too stunned to ask if she meant her entire class or just her group of friends. Either way, it was a startling announcement for this old Lubbock boy.

So, Gary and Barbara eventually D-I-V-O-R-C-E-D. Gary wound up in Austin, where he made an intense effort to change from being a reporter to a fiction writer. His novel, *The Hundred Yard War*, was published, but he found, as others before him had, that even having a pretty good novel published doesn't necessarily bring in enough money to support a family. By that time, Gary had remarried and was a father again.

Five or six nights a week, there was a party somewhere in Austin, and Gary and his new wife, Jo, didn't miss many. You have to LIVE to know what to write about, don't you? Sure you do. . . Live it up. . . Be there when IT happens. . .

I was there, too, most of the time. Commuting to Austin from Fort Worth and Dallas. . . . . You gotta be there because IT might happen the night you stay home to get some rest. . . Be there when it happens, man. That's what it's all about.

Cartwright had been a successful sportswriter and columnist in Dallas and something of a legendary figure in the minds of those Dallasites involved in the business end of professional football there—the players and coaches—as well as the fans. Cartwright wrote the not-soon-to-be-forgotten lead paragraph about the Four Horsemen of the Apocalypse in his game story of a Cowboys contest that ended with an intercepted Don Meredith pass on the opponent's goal line when a touchdown would have meant victory for the Cowboys. The lead started off something like this—as I don't have a copy at hand, this version may vary slightly, but the essence is here: "The Four Horsemen of the Apocalypse—you know them: Pestilence, War, Famine and Meredith . . ." This did not exactly endear Cartwright to Dandy Don, of course, or to some of Dandy's fans. But Dallas Cowboys fans who worshipped Don Meredith as an effective and colorful quarterback for the fledgling team also delighted in seeing one of pro sports' cockiest players get his comeuppance now and then.

Off duty, Cartwright was a founding member of the no doubt famous Flying Punzars, an acrobatic troupe that included Bud Shrake and Jerre Todd, another sportswriter who later went over to the money-making side of the journalism profession—Public Relations—and turned Republican. Todd had also been on Blackie Sherrod's sportswriting team at the old *Fort Worth Press* and the *Dallas Times-Herald*. The third slot on the Flying Punzars acrobatic team changed from time to time over the decades, for one reason or another, but Shrake and Cartwright were always there as the troupe's unstabilizing influence. The Flying Punzar's Dallas debut—in about 1960, as I recall—was at Dick Harp's 90th Floor saloon and jazz ha-

ven. There is no known written account of that breakthrough
event, and unfortunately details are sketchy at best, as the
memories of the participants, as well as the witnesses, long
ago went fuzzy.

I well remember a subsequent Flying Punzar appearance
in West Austin. It happened at a garden party in 1968. The
sky was cloudy all day and rain fell intermittently—time after time chasing the band with its electric instruments inside. Despite the conflicting protestations of fundamental
modesty, in the name of historical integrity, I must confess
here that I was an active member of the Flying Punzars acrobatic troupe on that rainy day on that hillside overlooking
Lake Travis. There was quite a crowd, as I recall, and we were
all three in full Punzar regalia. Cartwright and I had selected
and purchased the drapery material for our capes the previous day. We were planning to toss Cartwright's young son,
Shea, into the air for a triple flip as our grande finale. However, the rain continued to intrude, and every time the Flying
Punzars danced out in front of the band to begin our performance, the rain chased us back under the nearest shelter.

Finally, because of irresistible hunger pangs, I was forced
to remove my cape and tights and put my street clothes back
on so I could forage for food to satisfy a sudden sharp attack
of the munchies. It was shortly after that affair that Shrake
coined the now famous cautionary proverb: "A Punzar never
takes off his costume until he's done his act." I never again
performed as a member of the Flying Punzars. My spot in the
troupe, last I heard, had been filled by Jerry Jeff Walker.

A few weeks after she was sworn in as Governor of Texas
in 1991, Ann Richards told a *Dallas Morning News* reporter
about an evening, at a rather late hour, when Shrake and
Cartwright, accompanied by Jerry Jeff, showed up at her door,
dressed in tights and flowing robes, declaring themselves to

be the Flying Punzars, an acrobatic troupe. They tried repeatedly, Governor Richards said, to perform for her their famous triple flip, but failed miserably each and every time. I don't want to give the impression that I was, or am, vengeful or the least bit envious, but I was, and continue to be, rather pleased to hear they never were able to pull it off. As far as I know, in all the thirty-six or so years the Flying Punzars have been performing their act, they have never once managed to accomplish the triple flip. It has been somehow reassuring to me, I confess, to learn that they still hadn't been able to do it without me.

But I digress . . .

In the later 1960s, when Cartwright and other Maddogs were trying to choke creativity from mushrooms—both faux and natural—and pills of various hues, Jap was awarded a year at the J. Frank Dobie Ranch west of Austin by the Texas Institute of Letters. The idea of the award was to give promising Texas writers a time free from hassles—no rent to pay, no groceries to buy, no city hubbub to confront each day—just the beautiful hill country to inspire him or her and the ghost of J. Frank Dobie to commune with—accompanied by the music of cold spring water in the nearby Pedernales River gurgling over limestone boulders.

I don't know how much Gary managed to write while he was living at the Dobie Ranch with his wife, Jo and his son, Shea, but he did chat with Dobie. Had several conversations with the dearly departed folklorist, in point of fact, seated not far from the ranch house on a flat rock overlooking the Pedernales. How do I know this is true? Cartwright told me.

As mentioned earlier, while Jap and Jo were in residence at the Dobie Ranch, the Cartwrights hosted a semi-famous party during the week my wife of the moment and daughter, Carter, spent as their house guests. An Austin band, on its

way up or down—I don't remember which at this late date—
performed periodically for two days and nights. What seemed
to be hundreds of people of various and sundry persuasions
(all outfitted in the popular sixties mode of dress) were in
attendance.

Peter and Jodi Gent drove down from Dallas, and a gaggle
of movie people from California flew in for the festivities.
The California contingent included Dennis Hopper, who
starred in Shrake's *Kid Blue*. It didn't exactly boom at the box
office immediately, but it did attract a sort of cult following
over the years. The movie was filmed in Mexico, with the
Cartwrights and the Gents appearing as extras. Shrake himself had a mumbling bit part as the town drunk. Back in Dallas after the film shoot, Jodi Gent declared she had been a
movie star and she had not been a movie star, and she could
say, unequivocally, that she would rather be a movie star than
not be one. I was teaching at the time and was unable to flex
my schedule to get away for that particular trip to Mexico,
where I, no doubt, would have been a temporary movie star,
along with my fellow Maddogs. Timing, they say, is everything.

It was during the filming of *Kid Blue* that Dennis Hopper
was honored with his Maddog membership card, along with
Peter Boyle and producer Schwartz.

Coincidentally, the same weekend of the Cartwrights'
Dobie Ranch party and the visit by the California movie folks,
Willie Nelson's first July 4th picnic was held in a nearby pas-
ture. That was the first time veteran Maddogs heard the
musical poetry of future Maddogs Billy Joe Shaver and Steve
Fromholtz. The California crowd was duly impressed.

When Gary, Jo and Shea moved to Austin from Dallas,
they rented a house near the shores of Lake Travis. The nearest house to theirs was vacant and maybe a hundred yards or

so up a slight incline south of their brick, three-bedroom dwelling. Gary spent most of his time there working on *The Hundred Yard War*, although occasionally friends from Dallas and Austin interrupted his writing, enticing him away to join their parties. It must be added that Cartwright was seldom reluctant to push his work aside and take part in the so-called fun.

One afternoon, Gary answered a knock on his door to find two young men wearing clothes that could only be described as "hippie style." The spokesman of the pair, wearing shades and sporting a mustache, told Cartwright he and his buddy were considering renting the house up the hill and wondered if Gary knew how to contact the owner or agent. Cartwright said he had just moved in himself, but hoped they decided to take the place. "You look like our kind of folks," he declared, according to the mustachioed young man, although Gary has vehemently denied saying any such thing.

The pair turned out to be undercover narcs. During the trial months later, the clean shaven narc testified that, back in their car, his partner said, "Did you hear what he said? That we look like his kind of folks? Let's go back and have another look." Or words to that effect.

So they knocked on Cartwright's door again, and this time they asked if he knew where they could score some grass. Gary said no, he didn't, but he could help them out, and he went to a back room and brought out a single joint and offered it to the strangers. The mustachioed narc took the joint and offered Gary some money, which he refused—stuck it back into the narc's shirt pocket as he was leaving.

The next morning, before dawn, police busted into the Cartwright home and arrested Gary, dragging him away in handcuffs and leaving his wife stunned and their baby crying. The fact that Gary was something of a celebrity in certain circles even then caused his arrest to be reported on the news wires, and stories about the incident were printed in newspapers across Texas, including Dallas, where his name turned to mud with individuals and institutions that had loaned him money to buy his car and other modern day necessities. Those loans were immediately called in, further complicating the lives of the Cartwright family.

For giving an undercover agent a single marijuana cigarette out of the goodness of his heart, Gary Cartwright became a pariah. At least one U.S. president and many U.S. congressmen of both parties have since admitted experimenting with the killer weed during approximately that same period of time, but the sixties were perilous times for many an adventuresome youth in America. Not that they were all angels, but many who were caught in the general panic were less than criminals.

In the long run, it turned out reasonably well for Gary. Warren Burnet, the Odessa lawyer who already had made a name for himself on several fronts, took Cartwright's case *pro bono* (as another of his many contributions to the arts) and, following a brief hearing before a judge in Austin, the case was dismissed.

Burnet had asked me and H. G. Wells (the one from Tulia who had resigned his seat in the state legislature and moved his law practice to Fort Worth) to testify for Cartwright as character witnesses. We both agreed to do so without hesitation. All the way down on our drive to Austin that day we made up scenarios wherein our friend Cartwright was about to be strapped to the electric chair until we gave our testimony and then he was set free. As it turned out, we were never called on to testify and Cartwright got off anyway. But we were ready, like John Wayne, to ride to the rescue if needed.

Gary Cartwright, as most Texas fans of good writing are well aware by now, has become a successful magazine writer

(*Texas Monthly*) and an author of non-fiction books in the same league with such national best selling reporters as David Halberstam. Cartwright has, I think, surpassed—by a long shot, Bob Woodward of Watergate's investigative reporting fame, whose books lately have shown signs of pressing.

At some point in time, back in the mid-1970s, Cartwright seemed to disappear from the high-living scene in Austin. There were several more or less credible rumors, including one that he was working on a ditch-digging gang for the city to regain his health and sanity. Whatever Jap was doing during his incognito period, he came back stronger and healthier than ever, and more focused. Some gave much of the credit for Gary's revival to his new wife, Phyllis. He and Jo had been through too much, apparently, for that marriage to survive.

Last I heard, Gary and Phyllis had bought a house in Austin near the University and Gary was working on yet another book to follow the several already published during the eighties and early nineties. His byline during that time was frequently seen in large, bold letters on the covers of *Texas Monthly* magazine, where he was a Senior Editor.

Oh yes. Somewhere along in there Gary Cartwright survived triple bypass heart surgery and co-authored and co-produced with his old friend, Bud Shrake, a couple of network television movies starring Willie Nelson and Kris Kristofferson.

In the meantime, also, Cartwright's name was carved in brass and sunk into a sidewalk on Austin's Sixth Street, where it belongs, with the other Texas luminaries.

Not Enough Women To Go Around?

Speaking of women, and some of us often did back then, my friend Joe Murray, after listening to one of my tall tales about the Maddog and nights of the sixties and seventies, commented, "Looks to me like yawl didn't have enough women to go around."

I hadn't thought of it that way before, but I saw his point after mulling it over awhile.

I'm not sure why, but writers on every level, as a general thing, seem to have to marry A Lot of women in their lives. By A Lot I mean more than one or two. Three or four women, as some have married, is A Bunch, but more than one or two wives is just A Lot. I don't know if that's because writers need specific kinds of women, or what.

I do remember a story I heard about John Steinbeck, who married Elaine, a sister of Jean Anderson Boone, who grew up in Fort Worth and was a cousin, or some kin, of Dan Jenkins or his wife. I forget which, if I ever knew. Anyway, Jean's sister Elaine married Steinbeck when they were both past their physical primes, as they say, and both had been married before. When their honeymoon was over and they moved into Steinbeck's house in New England, the Nobel Prize-winning author wanted his new bride to be in the house while he was upstairs in his office writing. Not just in the neighborhood, but in the house.

At first, Elaine was flattered by her famous new husband's devotion. But after a month or two, it got boring staying in the house all day while he was upstairs, out of touch with her, having all that fun writing stuff thousands of people would soon be reading and thinking how wonderful he was to have written it. So, one day, about mid-week before they were to have guests over the coming weekend, Elaine decided to run into the nearby village to buy the stuff she needed to feed and entertain their guests and she told Steinbeck of her plans, thinking he would understand, surely, that doing her errands now would save having to rush like hell late Friday evening or Saturday morning to do everything she had to get done before their guests arrived.

But, to Elaine's surprise and considerable chagrin, Steinbeck said no. He wanted her in the house.

"That's silly, honey," she said—or something to that effect. "All I'm trying to do is get ready for our weekend guests."

"All I'm trying to do is write a book," he answered firmly. So, she stayed in the house.

I think maybe most men and women who consider themselves serious writers—that being all men and women who are trying to write—would understand what Steinbeck was saying. They might not require that their spouse stay in the house while they try to write, but conditions probably have to be a certain, specific way for the writing to flow as it should. That alone could explain why so many writers have had so many wives. (I omit women writers here, because I don't know about them; their demons may be similar to those plagued by males, but someone else will have to tell us about that.)

I've had only one novel published—and a number of magazine pieces and news features—but I think of myself as a Writer. I agree with Gary Cartwright, who once said if you think of yourself as a writer and try to write, you are a Writer. You may not be a successful writer, but you are a Writer. The measure of your success is determined by a number of factors besides the fact that you actually write, although that is the prime consideration. You aren't a Writer if you just say you are one and don't ever get around to writing anything. But whether or not you actually publish a best-selling novel has nothing to do with whether or not you are a Writer.

So, anyway, I consider myself a Writer and I know that conditions must be Just Right for me to produce publishable pages of prose. I don't mean I have to wait for inspiration; that's not where it's at. What I mean is that my life must be reasonably free from internal or external problems or I can't build up enough of the total concentration it takes for me to write well—to have the confidence to produce a creative work and believe that what I have created is good enough to let someone else read it. Just as in athletics, dance, acting, painting, or whatever, it takes both confidence and concentration to produce something worthwhile—in writing prose or poetry, performing artistically, or playing a good game of football or basketball or golf, for that matter.

When my life is the least bit screwed up somehow, I can't write anything but journalism. In many ways, because my life has been screwed up more often than not, most of my literary endeavors have wound up as journalism. And the main reason my life has been more or less screwed up throughout my adulthood, is women. Well, that's not really fair, I suppose. I should say I've been more or less screwed up all my adult life mainly because of my attitude toward women. All my wrong-headed ideas about them.

For instance, I thought for years that if you slept with a woman you had to ask her to marry you. That mistaken belief I attribute to several childhood disadvantages, and the fact that I am a card-carrying member of the Big War generation, which was definitely a pre-1960s generation in regard to its sensibilities regarding women. Strangely enough, I did seem to fit into the sixties in other ways, despite my age. I was teaching journalism on college campuses during that pivotal decade and found myself in sync with my students more than with my administrators. This did not particularly endear me to my administrators, but it did to my students. Or most of them. I still hear from some of them, and that pleases me.

It seems to me some of my friends who are Writers, most of whom have achieved more success at it than I, feed off internal and external problems in their lives. The more screwed up his life was, or used to be, the more good, really funny stuff Larry L. King would turn out.

Bud Shrake somehow churned out books, screenplays, as-told-to biographies and magazine pieces—regardless of the situation at home, or how late the hour or how much fermented liquid he had managed to swallow the night before.

Women never seemed to bother Shrake. Of course, I don't know that for certain. No one, except Shrake himself, does. But regardless of his relationships with women, he managed to keep on turning out a copious body of admirable professional work over the years.

Willie Nelson wrote many of his best songs back when his life was in chaos. He said one time, after his career was rolling in high cotton, that it wasn't easy to write good sad songs when you were flying to your gigs in a private jet.

"Mr. Bojangles," as most everyone knows by now, was inspired by Jerry Jeff Walker's incarceration in a New Orleans jail. Matter of fact, Walker is possibly the contemporary songwriter with the most personal body of work. All of his songs are about his own life and experiences, real or imagined. This method obviously works for Jerry Jeff in happy times, as well as times of tribulation. If you play Walker's albums in chronological order, you will discover his life history, from his rambling scrambling days on the road to his more peaceful times as a husband and father. Jerry Jeff has been married more than once, but when he married Susan more than twenty years ago, he hit the jackpot as far as a perfect match goes.

But, once again, apparently, I digress . . .

As I was saying, propelled by the mistaken belief that every woman a man slept with expected him to propose marriage, I wound up marrying women who didn't suit me, nor I them, and the results were inevitable. I have always been hardheaded about where I want to go and how I want to get there, and in spite of a few side trips that never lasted very long, I always wound up back on the track.

I don't mean to imply that I was always the perfect mate. I'm big enough to admit I'm not perfect. (See how perfect I am?) My excuse has been that I grew up in an era when, ostensibly, at least, the man of the house was the boss and, if not, then the man of the house was a wimp or whatever wimps were called back in those long-ago times. Henpecked. Or whatever. This silly charade provided much of the comic material for feature movies and TV series. Father always either knew best or was a goofus and everybody else in the family knew more than he did. Neither was true, of course, but somebody in charge of TV and movies and comic strips apparently figured this was America's fantasy life. Now that I think about it, maybe those TV and movie and comic strip moguls actually thought the nation's wives and children wanted to see father portrayed as either all wise or idiotic because they really seemed to be like that—either A or B. Who knows—maybe their asinine analysis was a causal factor for the widespread family problems today.

Anyhow, after several mismatches, both official and unofficial, I at last realized that what I really needed was a female partner who already had her own thing going and going good. It seemed to me I was always winding up with women who didn't know who they were or where they were going and who, therefore, somehow ended up wanting to be me. Sooner or later, the women in my life all seemed to come to the conclusion I was having more fun than they were, and that what I was doing looked so easy they could do it too, and better than I was doing it. What they didn't seem to understand was it had taken me a lot of years to get where I could make it look that easy. Possibly one of the things about writing that fools a lot of people is that it looks so easy. People are always coming up to me and saying, "Boy, have I got a story to tell if I just had the time (or patience, or whatever) to sit down and write it." As if all it takes is time.

In those boss/non-boss relationships of the olden days, the non-boss had to get sneaky. "Don't let the boss catch me doing this or that or find out I did it or was about to do it!" You can imagine the kind of relationship such deviousness would tend to promote. A dishonest one, at the very least. But it seems to me that wives, down through the Judeo-Christian ages, have needed to develop a certain amount of sneakiness to keep the family functioning. The manner, range and motives of the wife's sneakiness was what made the marriage heaven or hell, or a little or a lot of both.

We're still working on perfecting a better relationship system—one wherein the husband and wife are equal partners. Some couples are able to manage that arrangement and others can't do it. Or won't—for many reasons, most of them having to do with how the man or woman was raised.

One problem I've had to rassle with most of my life (until relatively recently, that is) has to do with the fact (yes, the fact) that many women, especially young women, are often more attracted to Rascals than they are to Nice Boys. Due, perhaps at least in part, to a certain ingrained mental cowardice—or maybe actual physical cowardice, or fear of pain or embarrassment, with hopefully at least a small element of basic goodness in there—I was classified, in high school, particularly, and to some extent in college, as a Nice Boy. It became clear to me, sometimes years later and sometimes on the spot, that an alarming number of attractive young women were turned off by Nice Boys. Or maybe they were just turned on by Rascals. A bemusing set of circumstances. I don't know if my reputation as a Nice Boy really was, ultimately, a plus or a minus in my life, but there were times I felt it was a definite minus. I was much younger then, of course.

It has occurred to me that the wives and sweethearts of the Texas writers of prose and music I have known who lasted any length of time were either extraordinarily strong-minded, or more than a little bit masochistic. The extraordinarily strong-minded women usually established themselves as individual personalities in the group, while the masochists, as often as not, were more or less destroyed—sometimes literally. Others, of course, simply disappeared from the group for some reason. Maybe to save themselves. Or maybe just because they wanted to.

The fact is, despite being sensitive in many areas of their thinking, prose and music writers I've known have tended to be more than slightly chauvinistic as far as women were concerned. The attitudes and behavior of some of them sometimes were perceived by their women as fundamentally abusive—psychologically if not physically. Sometimes the women found such chauvinism interesting, and sometimes boring, depending, I suppose, on the woman and the circumstances.

There is a theory with some validity, if you look at it from certain points of view, that women who throw themselves, sexually, at writers or performers are asking to be treated badly, or should expect to be. I've always been puzzled by the fact so many women appear to turn into raging, sex-starved fanatics by some fellow standing on a stage and singing poetry into a microphone. (Could that be because I can't sing on key?) But no kidding, what is it about singing into a microphone that's so sexually stimulating to so many women? I just don't get it. My reaction to this phenomenon is much the same as that of Billy Joe Shaver regarding homosexual men. "I know there's such a thing as queers," Shaver told me one day. "I just can't grasp it in my mind." This observance from a fellow who had written some of the most sensitive poetry in country rock music.

There were always groupies following Texas singer/songwriters I have known. And not all of them were female. Some were male hustlers—procuring dope or women or both for the performers they seemed to idolize. Some of them were there to perform whatever task or obtain whatever thing the performer wanted or needed at the moment—a sandwich, space to walk through a throng of fans—or whatever their idol desired. There was one guy who used to dress like Willie and travel with him everywhere, from town to town, bounding out ahead of Willie and yelling, "Make room! Make room!" Then there was this doctor who . . . well, he wound up serving prison time for providing musicians with various prescription drugs. This friendly physician was also known from time to time to hand out prescriptions to female groupies and arrange orgies with them and his musical heroes. These services got him backstage and earned him the apparent devotion of the stars. Someone asked him one day why he followed musicians around all the time. "Well," he said, "I don't play golf."

I met Willie Nelson after a show in Dallas the night he sang the entire album, *Phases and Stages*, and I was forever hooked as a Willie fan. Gene McCoslin, who managed the joint where Willie playcd that night, was a former member of Willie's traveling "Family" and had called me repeatedly, trying to get me to come out some night and interview Willie for *Iconoclast*, the Dallas weekly alternative paper I found myself editing at the time. Geno was sure that if Willie was introduced to the *Iconoclast* audience of lingering hippie types and college professors (this was 1973), it would contribute to an important breakthrough for his music. As it turned out, Geno's theory was true, in spades.

For reasons hard to explain, after that first meeting, Willie and I became friends. He would call me when he was scheduled to play somewhere he thought might be an interesting scene, or one fairly close to Dallas, and I usually wound up hanging out backstage with him and Paul and Mickey Raphael and others in his band. It was fun, and I was writing a lot of articles for *Iconoclast* and other publications based on those backstage experiences. The other singer/songwriters I met along the way would talk to me because they figured if I was Willie's friend, I must be okay.

Hanging out with Willie was always interesting and, more often than not, downright enjoyable. That reminds me of a bumper sticker somebody distributed around Austin in the mid-seventies that said something like: "If You're Good, When You Die You Get to Go to Willie's House; If You're Bad, You Have to Go to David Allen Coe's."

But the more popular Willie and his music became, the less fun it was for me to be around him and the band. The worst part was I began to feel like a groupie myself. I remember one particular night backstage before a show in Waco, when a middle-aged female fan found her way back where Willie was relaxing. Just him and me in this vast backstage area in some kind of convention center. We were just sitting there, not even talking, when she walked in and poured her worshipfulness all over Willie, who sat smiling his Willie smile and politely answering her questions.

Finally, she seemed to run low on steam and turned to me and asked, "Are you anybody?"

I couldn't come up with an answer. I thought about her question later that night and for several days afterward. It wasn't long before I stopped following Willie around.

Some of the groupies pursuing the singers who wrote their own songs would settle for going to bed with some guy in the band, if the star who wrote and sang was otherwise occupied, or simply passed them by. Others, probably those who either were rejected by the band or figured getting to know a pal of the main man would get them closer to him than bedding a band member, would sometimes make a move on a male groupie, or a buddy of the singer whose presence backstage seemed to make him appear to be a groupie—as I had begun to fear my presence there did. I've been approached by female groupies who thought I was a close buddy of Willie's or Jerry Jeff's or Billy Joe Shaver's, and they seemed to figure, "what the hey, maybe if I bed down with this fellow, it'll lead me one step closer to the star." They never came right out and said so specifically, of course, but I always suspected it was true and, therefore, could never respond to any of them. Not a single one, regardless of how attractive—and some of them were very attractive, although this was not always the case. Pride, as they say, goeth before going without, but if that kind of pride exists, there is little or nothing a person can do about it short of getting very drunk, which, as I have mentioned previously, I seldom managed to do because of that very same pride, which somehow involved the persistent fear of making an ass of myself.

The pecking order of backstage groupies, male and female, nevertheless, seemed to me a fascinating social phenomenon. As for my friend Joe Murray's observation that the Maddog Group of Texas writers apparently didn't have enough women to go around, I've thought about it at some length and come to the conclusion that what might seem in the telling to be a noteworthy number of women moving from one man to another within that circle, wasn't really unique to the Maddog Group.

Oh, there was one time Fletcher and Dorothy (Billie Lee Brammer's wife) ran off together to New York City, so much in love of each other, it was bigger than both of them. Seems Billie Lee and Dorothy and Fletcher and Jean had been hanging out together a lot, playing bridge and going to movies and so forth, which apparently ignited the first spark of love that turned into a blazing fire so hot they couldn't stand it no more. Once they were in New York, Fletcher planned to become a famous artist with the help of his friends Bud Shrake and Dan Jenkins, who had been in Gotham awhile by then, and had connections, you know.

For reasons one can only imagine, Fletcher and Dorothy's great passion lasted only about two weeks and Fletcher was soon back in Austin. Dorothy eventually married another Texas writer, Jan Reid.

And come to think of it, Shrake's first wife, Joyce, later married a lawyer friend of mine in Fort Worth, Sheridan Taylor, although Sheridan, who died of cancer in the early 1980s, wasn't a Maddog—not officially, anyway. A friend of Shrake's—the first real hippie I ever met in person—who'd been staying with Shrake in New York—headed back to Texas and at Shrake's particular request went by to see Shrake's former wife and his children, all then living with Taylor. Joyce Shrake Taylor wound up running off to Santa Fe with the aforementioned authentic hippie friend of Bud's, leaving Taylor in the lurch, so to speak, although I've never been sure what "in the lurch" meant.

Dan Jenkins's first wife was a former Fort Worth Paschal High girl, Joan Holloway. They were married for awhile and Joan, a strong-minded woman, continued as a Maddog possible for a time until she went over to the conservatives after working in Govenor John Connally's administration long enough to be contaminated.

I lived for awhile in a guest house located on Joan's parents' property on a hill southwest of Austin. It was at the Holloway's that I first met Sheridan Taylor, who was an admirer of Joan Holloway Jenkins at the time, and who later married Joyce Shrake, who ran off to New Mexico with . . . well, I just told you that story.

The same night I met lawyer Taylor at Joan Holloway Jenkins's house on the hill overlooking Austin, he was with another lawyer, H. G. Wells—the one from Tulia—who was an old Army buddy of Gary Cartwright's and later moved to Fort Worth and, eventually, married lawyer Taylor's widow, Sheila Taylor, who wrote one of the most popular feature columns ever run in the *Fort Worth Star-Telegram*.

Oh, yes. There was the young woman we called Jungle Girl—a real beauty who said very little in the early days, when she was, it turned out, still a student at the University. Some thought she was just a dumb bimbo because she was so reserved. She lived with Fletcher for awhile, then after she graduated she moved to Dallas and told me then that, at that point, I was the only writer Maddog she hadn't bedded down.

And, of course, I can't fail to mention in this regard the interesting fact that Billie Lee Brammer's first ex-wife, Nadine, married Bob Eckhardt, who was perhaps Billie Lee's number one political hero and a model for at least one of the protagonists in *The Gay Place*. Eckhardt was in the Texas legislature then, a leader of the liberal rebels who always fought the good fight but seldom won—in other words, the real-life prototypes of the political rebels in Billie Lee's novel. That Nadine married Eckhardt is, you might say, ironic. So is the fact that, after Nadine and Eckhardt split, Willie Morris's ex-wife Celia, married Bob Eckhardt.

And so it goes. Or went.

I'm sure there were other matches and cross-matches I didn't know about, but I still contend this Maddog Group of writers and their women were no more sexually indiscriminate than any group of "regular" people whose gathering place is, say, a local country club. Something similar occurs, I'm pretty sure, among the workers in your average office where half a dozen or more are employed.

Maybe I'm naive—or would this direction of thinking be called cynical? Or maybe the difference between the Maddog Group of writers—who seem to divorce a lot—and members of the country club bunch, is merely that the writers, for whatever reason, are more inclined to go ahead and get divorced.

Then there's what you might call the Elizabeth Taylor theory: that people who wed many times do so because they believe you ought to marry the people you sleep with.

Or the whole thing could be June Allyson's fault.

Austin and
Its Music

They worked hard and hustled and worked hard some more until they've damn near ruined Austin, which used to be, arguably, the best little city in America, at least.

Austin still attracts writers and artists and musicians and other nuts, so all is not entirely lost. It's still there, but now you have to look for it, or know somebody who knows where it is. Any place that puts down sidewalk monuments enshrining football heroes, picker poets and crazy writers before it similarly honors a former President of the United States of America who grew up nearby and spent a lot of time there can't be all bad. Austin is still a place that doesn't execute citizens who fight growth. They're still there, too, albeit in a shrinking minority and (as usual) more easily distracted and less organized than their worker bee opposites who keep trying so hard to spoil the very essence of what made Austin such a fine place to live in the first place.

As Jerry Jeff Walker, a prominent Austin immigrant, once discerningly pointed out: "All roads lead into Austin and roads going everywhere else go right out from there." That's the reason, Jerry Jeff said, he decided to settle down there in the early 1970s.

The biggest changes have happened—no, "happened" is the wrong word here—these changes haven't just happened; they've been engineered, finagled, masterminded, hustled— they have been deliberately brought about by people who actually believe as Govenor Bush claimed to when he said, "There's no such thing as too much growth."

I say "claimed to" believe, because it's hard for me to swallow that an intelligent person could really give credence to that idea.

When I go to Austin nowadays, I always think about what a neighbor of ours in Lubbock, Mr. George, said one day when we stood watching a beat-up old station wagon roll past with arms waving and kids screaming from every window. "That feller just about screwed hisself out of a seat," Mr. George observed dryly. I think about Mr. George's comment every time I try to drive through Dallas, or Houston, or even parts of Fort Worth and other Texas cities—even Austin—where, in the not so distant past, one could get from one place to another by automobile relatively easily.

Take Arlington, for example. Arlington used to be this really nice, quiet, little college town, but some local business people worked and studied and maneuvered and planned and finally managed to turn that once perfectly nice, quiet little college town into a exasperating replica of some East coast suburban hell: a sprawl of apartments and congested traffic— always in the top ten for stolen automobiles and assorted big city crimes against property and persons and a population as transitory as a gypsy camp in Hungary—or wherever it is that gypsy camps are prevalent.

But, hallelujah! In spite of the Philistines, Austin has managed to remain the kind of place where good live music can be found almost any evening in more than one place. More than one kind of really superior music, in fact, in more than one Austin-kind-of-place.

And best of all—it's music that still concentrates on the picking and not the fireworks—or whatever—that can be concocted around the picking. It's my theory the curse of good music is the music video revolution and its influence on live music. When I listen to music, I don't like being distracted by burning guitars and fancy costumes and staged sound and visual effects exploding and flashing all around the musicians. I want to see talented pickers walk out on the stage and pick and sing good music, straight ahead, with a minimum of talk, and absolutely none whatsoever of what has come to be regarded as "showmanship."

I don't mind a little prancing around, à la Mick Jagger, because the Rolling Stones's emphasis has always been on the picking. But my favorite kind of music shows are those done by Willie, Jerry Jeff, Bonnie Raitt, Eric Clapton, et al, who simply walk out there in more or less regular attire and hold your attention with good music and lyrics that make sense because you can relate to what they say. Call me old fogy, but I sense that melody and lyrics are slowly making their comeback. Hopefully, it's true in music, as well as other things, that what goes around comes around.

Austin is not perfect, of course, and it never has been. One of its eternal problems is that because so many people want to live there, salaries are lower than they ought to be since people are willing to work for less just for the pleasure of living in Austin. And it's no longer cheap to live there—if it ever was.

That reminds me of one night a few years ago, in my Austin apartment when my friends Fletcher and Jean Boone, before their divorce, got into a lengthy and rather noisy argu-

ment about whether or not they should leave Austin for a
better opportunity elsewhere. In Rome. The Rome in Italy, as
a matter of fact. Jean had been offered a job by the Lyndon B.
Johnson people in Rome. Best I recall, it had something to do
with the Voice of America office there. Jean wanted to take
the job, and Fletcher, who was concentrating on being a painter
and sculptor at the time, was surprisingly against the move,
for reasons he was disinclined to make clear.

To better understand what was at stake here for both parties, you should know that Fletcher and Jean, in those days,
were one of the most popular (for lack of a better descrip-
tion) couples in town. At least among the liberal *Observer*
crowd. Back then in Texas, in matters political, the conservatives and liberals stuck to themselves, philosophically speaking. But when it came to partying in Austin—as it frequently
did—there was more than a little blurring of the lines between
the two factions. In other words, many individuals of both
philosophical persuasions often mixed and mingled together
at social affairs in various private homes and public watering
holes around town. Austin was, especially during legislative
sessions, one of the best party towns in Texas, if not the entire country. Not a few members of the state legislature repeatedly ran for re-election for that reason alone—or so I hear.

Anyhow, that night in my apartment, Fletcher and Jean
were debating the pros and cons of accepting Jean's job offer
in Rome, where—as Jean kept emphasizing, Fletcher would
be exposed to some of the world's greatest art, as well, no
doubt, as other contemporary artists with plenty to say and
show. Although I would have missed them both, I had to agree
with Jean and argue her side against Fletcher's. The proposed
move just looked to me to be the right thing for them to do.
Seemed to me living in Rome would be more advantageous
for Fletcher, in fact, than it would be for Jean, whose job there,

as I recall, would be fairly routine. The Boones' argument had been going back and forth, off and on, since early evening and was taken up again after we left whatever party we had attended and stopped by my apartment to wind the evening down. Finally the argument reached the real moment of truth when Fletcher said: "Okay. Okay. But what about the parties?"

"What do you mean, what about the parties?" Jean asked.

"I mean the parties in Rome. We'll be just one more American government employee and one more aspiring artist over there. We're not movie stars or millionaires. We won't be invited to the best parties like we are in Austin."

At that, Jean was more or less speechless, and the Boones soon left my apartment.

Next morning very early, I was awakened from a deep, restorative sleep by the loud voices of my neighbors on the other side of my bedroom wall. It didn't take long to realize the couple had taken up Fletcher and Jean's argument where they had left off the night before. The guy strongly agreed with Fletcher, and she declared loudly that Jean's position was the only one that made sense.

The Boones, by the way, stayed in Austin—until their divorce several years later. Jean eventually wound up in New York City working for one of those big TV network game shows. Fletcher teamed up with his boyhood chum Jim (Lopez) Smithum and opened the Raw Deal, which was one of the "In" places in Austin for a number of years until the partners split up and Fletcher opened Another Raw Deal or Raw Deal Too and Lopez stayed with the original Raw Deal on Sixth Street downtown. Fletcher married Libby, a wonderful woman, who died a few years later. "Unexpectedly," as they say. Perhaps Fletcher's most remarkable attribute, according to many of his friends, was his mysterious attraction to such really great women. But that's a whole other story.

● ● ●

In the 1960s, Willie Nelson, a native of Abbott, Texas, was still working out of Nashville where he'd gone to seek his fortune as a singer/songwriter—just as so many had before him. He started selling his songs right away, but Nashville music honchos never seemed to go for his singing. They said he sang out of meter. They had said the same thing about another Texan, Roger Miller, before his surprise hit album in the early sixties, the one that included "Chugalug" and "Kansas City Star" and all those other off-beat songs that made Miller a national phenomenon almost overnight.

"People kept telling me to just stay up in the hills and write songs for other people to sing," Willie told me years later. "If I had, there never would have been a Willie Nelson."

Meantime, at North Texas State University in Denton, an English Literature professor named Stan Alexander organized a folk music club that attracted talented students such as Steve Fromholz, B. W. Stevenson, Michael Murphy and Ray Wylie Hubbard. And at about the same time, a lanky guitar-picking gypsy from upper New York state (named Paul Crosby)—who renamed himself Jerry Jeff Walker—was wandering in and out of Texas and attending some guitar pulls, as jam sessions were sometimes called, along with Townes Van Zandt, Guy Clark and other Texas songwriters and aspiring songwriters. A University of Texas student from Port Arthur named Janis Joplin was imitating Bessie Smith on Sundays at Kenneth Threadgill's Austin place, singing for nothing but the experience. Young pickers named Gary P. Nunn, John Inmon, Bob Livingston, and others were moving through rock and roll toward their deeper roots.

At the same time, George Jones, Ernest Tubb, Loretta Lynn, Buck Owens and other traditional country stars were still packing them in along the "Grits Circuit" which included Panther Hall in Fort Worth, Dallas's Longhorn Ballroom, Austin's Skyline Ballroom, Lubbock's Cotton Club, Gruene Hall near Austin, and other strictly starched white shirt/big hat joints around the state, their parking lots loaded with pickup trucks.

The audience Willie encountered in Texas was ready for his rock-oriented music and intelligent lyrics. Consciously or not, they had been getting ready most of their lives. Willie's music was basically country, but more. And, from the other direction, this new, younger audience had been hearing some of the best of their rock era musical heroes—Dylan, Grateful Dead, Byrds, Poco, The Band, Nitty Gritty Dirt Band and others—edging toward their country roots for some time. But a major problem had been that no established country stars had been willing, or able, to appreciate what these younger pickers were attempting to accomplish—a new, all-American music, firmly rooted in folk and country attitudes and sounds, but improved, not diluted, by sounds and viewpoints from more modern aspects of updated living experiences. There was still in the atmosphere a residue of the social and political fragmentation of the 1960s.

By the time Willie and his people moved their operation back home to Texas in the winter of 1973, the Texas music scene had reached the point where it needed a special component to make it come together into something it had been edging toward for so long. A new breed of country musician had been coming of age, a generation young enough and sensitive enough in the rocking sixties to know that country music could be better if it had more than three chords and delved deeper with its lyrics than a minnow's plunge.

That special ingredient was provided by the music and the presence of Willie Nelson "and family." Among other things, Willie provided a rocklike Survivor Image to cling to—strong, often-bludgeoned, but unbowed, a still smiling symbol of the past—standing solid and benevolent in their midst. Teaching by example only—never preaching—and always learning as well. Willie never changed. His music seemed to encompass the past, present and future. Older fans understood Willie's music, but there was now also something else happening out there. His physical appearance, his tolerance for sincere ideas coming from all directions, even his progressive ideas regarding certain mind-altering potions—caused Willie to be seen as a rebel, and this appealed to the young rock and roll crowd. And, amazingly, it didn't turn away his older fans. A few were bothered when he let his hair grow long—but those who complained weren't the ones really listening anyway.

Willie's band included Paul English, who had played drums with Willie since his Fort Worth days as a radio singer and volunteer Sunday School teacher. ("Paul's brother had been sitting in on drums for me and one day, he couldn't make it, so he got his brother, Paul, who played trumpet in a Salvation Army band, to sit in, and he's been with me ever since." Paul English, of course, is the Paul of Willie's song "Me and Paul." He's also the devil in Leon Russell's song, "You Look Like the Devil.")

And there was Bee Spears, who had played bass for Willie since he was a teenager. Willie's sister, Bobbie, played piano, and Mickey Raphael, a city boy from Dallas, had moved into his place on harmonica when Willie and the band were playing at a Big D joint called the Western Place, run at the time by a former Willie road manager, Gino McCoslin, who later would do most of the organizing of Willie's annual Fourth of July Picnics.

Willie "and family" were introduced to Austin music lovers at Armadillo World Headquarters, the first so-called "country" band to play that monolith of rock and roll and shrine to hippieness. In Dallas, at McCoslin's Western Place, Willie was interviewed by the local alternative weekly, *Iconoclast*, and when they played a benefit performance broadcast over the local public television station, Willie Nelson and the family were immediately embraced by the young Dallas longhaired rock and rollers as their very own.

In those years, as some of you are old enough to recall, male rock and roll hippies wore long hair and male so-called rednecks wore their hair short. That was one way you could tell them apart. A longhaired male in a country juke joint was often in danger of getting his ass whipped, or worse. So, when Willie played the Western Place in Dallas and the room began to fill with the potentially volatile combination of longhaired hippie types and starched white-shirted redneck types—the hippies and their bra-less dates, with long ironed-straight hair, all crowded together with the big-hatted rednecks' big-haired womenfolk in knee-length square dance dresses—the manager of the Western Place, who had gone to a lot of trouble to book Willie and make sure the show was advertised in *Iconoclast* and other papers read by college students, began to get a little bit nervous. More than just a little bit nervous, I should say, since McCoslin was the naturally nervous type to begin with. But largely, if not exclusively, due to Willie's calming influence, there was not a single flare-up of violence during the entire three-night stand there. The crowds seemed somewhat amazed themselves. The third night, Willie announced he had just made a new album, and asked the crowd if they would like to hear it. There was a loud, YESSSS! in answer, of course, and Willie told the crowd they would have to be quiet because all the songs put together told a story. Everyone moved in as close to the stage as possible, and many sat on the dance floor to listen. Then Willie played and sang all the songs, in order, from his album *Phases and Stages*.

Before that night at the Western Place in Dallas, I had not been a Willie fan. But hearing that album, done live, hooked me good. I started listening then, and have been listening ever since. If you really listen, and if you're not tone deaf, you'll become a Willie fan.

Anyhow, this was along about the same time that what was sometimes called the "Texas music uprising" began to take shape and attract attention beyond the borders of the Lone Star State. Picker poets with something to say were moving to Austin or booking gigs there as often as they could get them, despite the low pay. The money might not have been so good, but the audiences were gloriously understanding. Jerry Jeff Walker and his Lost Gonzo Band were probably the best known nationally in the early 1970s.

Jerry Jeff was making his own songs (along with the songs of Guy Clark, who hadn't started performing seriously at that time), well known all around the country, but particularly in Texas. Soon picker poets either working out of Austin or passing through regularly included such extraordinary talents as Lee Clayton, the Lubbock native who lived mostly in California but wrote songs that were recorded regularly by Willie, Jerry Jeff and Waylon. Clayton, with his unique circle-back style, had developed his own audience following the release of an album and occasional personal appearances. And there were: Asleep at the Wheel, whose Western Swing was about as close as a young bunch could get to Bob Wills's sound; and Doug Sahm, who had returned to Texas after conquering the San Francisco music scene with his Sir Douglas Quintet; and

Billy Joe Shaver, the primitive genius songwriter from Corsicana, who provided all the songs for a popular Waylon album *Honky Tonk Heroes*, followed by his own album, *Old Five and Dimers*, produced by fellow Texan, Kris Kristofferson; and Ray Wylie Hubbard, whose "Redneck Mother" became something of an anthem for the Texas music uprising, since just about all the bands did it in their stage shows (as an answer, it was said, to Merle Haggard's "Okie from Muskogee"); and George M. Jones, the Dallas picker poet with the warped sense of humor, who, when I asked him why he didn't change his name, answered, "Why in the world would I do that?" And Billy C., whose haunting song, "Hands on the Wheel," was picked by Willie to conclude his monster hit album, *Red Headed Stranger*.

And Townes Van Zandt, who was the inspiration for most of the other Texas songwriters; and Danny Epps, whose lifestyle kept him from being up there with the very best of the bunch; and Guy Clark, who went on to become the dean of Nashville songwriters; and Kinky Friedman, who described his own offbeat music as "country with a conscience"; and Johnny Darrell, whose early hits included "Ruby, Don't Take Your Love to Town" and "Green Green Grass of Home"; and Alvin Crow and Rusty Weir and Dee Moeller and Milton Carroll; and, of course, Kenneth Threadgill, whose bell-like yodel brought back memories of Jimmie Rodgers. And the Fort Worth blues genius, Delbert McClinton and his sidekicks. And others whose names don't come back immediately to my memory at the moment—which is too bad, because they were all worth listening to. Some have disappeared and others have stuck to their guns and are doing all right, in Texas and in other places all around the country, along with a whole new generation of musicians and performers who were inspired by those old bulls named above (pardon me, ladies).

The Texas music uprising of the seventies changed country music, all right—at least for awhile.

Back in those exhilarating times, the best nights for listeners and pickers alike were when more than one of the bunch were in town at the same time, playing in different joints, and running back and forth to pick with each other and getting together after hours to keep the excitement rolling. It was not always easy to keep up with them on those marvelous musical nights, but it was worth the trouble and the wear and tear on your body and mind to be up as close as possible to the creative energies generated as they invented their music right there before our very eyes and ears.

I was fortunate enough, when this amazing music uprising was happening, to be spending considerable time with Willie and others at the center of the revolution—writing about it for various publications and publishing the programs for Willie's annual Fourth of July Picnics. I worked mostly out of Dallas then, and down in Austin, it was—looking back on it—inevitable that Shrake, Cartwright and other writers I knew were becoming friends with the Austin-based picker poets—Willie and Jerry Jeff in particular. It was inevitable because they were all cut from the same cloth. Some could sing, and others wrote their thoughts and feelings down to be read. It had to do—the difference, I mean—with having perfect pitch or not. Those with perfect pitch chose to sing what they wrote. Those whose ears were not so well-tuned had to (didn't necessarily choose to, that is) be satisfied with not putting their words to music. The point is they were so very much alike in so many other ways, they naturally gravitated toward each other. As Billy Joe Shaver once put it, "water seeks its own level."

So, I was startled and delighted when, while reading Emmett Grogan's autobiographical novel, *Ringolevio*, I ran across this passage that seemed to me to describe precisely those prose writers and picker poets I knew:

> They are individuals, families, gangs who are bound together by the blues life . . . the ones who survive the plagues. . . . The best music— the best of everything that is expressive of all this country's got to give is by and about them . . . . [They are] the only ones who had reached their own rock bottom and got up. . . . They searched for brothers and sisters, not friends. . . . They didn't sell their vision—to sell their vision would have been to pretend it was theirs. . . . They were all innocent. They were felons. . . . They loved. They were the offspring of the mid-twentieth century broken consciousness. They were beyond the possibility of defeat. . . . Nothing moves a mountain but itself. . . .

And they are still there in Austin, if you know where to look.

Stumbling Toward a Fall

I had felt so bad that when I got to feeling almost normal I didn't realize I was still sick because I felt so much better than I had just before that. I thought I felt pretty good, in fact, when the truth was I was slipping dangerously low into a black hole of Depression.

I didn't recognize it as Depression with a capital D for a long time. This was before Depression got to be so popular it was on all the TV talk shows. But things had happened, bad things—after I returned home to Texas in 1961. Before that, just about everything I'd ever done had turned out the way I'd hoped, or better. I'd had what cops in crime novels call a "Rabbi" on every newspaper I'd worked for and even at the high school where I had coached three years after graduating from college. By "Rabbi" I mean a guy—it was always a guy—who kind of looked out for me, who seemed to like me enough and believe in me enough to make sure I didn't screw up too bad, or if I did screw up he'd smooth things out for me because he believed in me.

Therefore, things had always gone at least as well as I expected and, as often as not, better than I'd dared hope.

My private life hadn't gone all that beautifully. What I'm talking about here is my professional life. My career, you might say, had progressed at a satisfyingly rapid clip. By the time I was thirty-five I had moved from a small daily in a small town in south Mississippi to the editorial page of the *New York Herald Tribune* (by way of the managing editor's job at Hodding Carter's Pulitzer Prize winning daily in the Mississippi delta), sold a novel to a New York publisher and made a favorable impression on my bosses at the *Herald Tribune.*

When I returned to the Lone Star State, I kept writing columns for the *Herald Tribune*'s editorial page whenever I came up with an idea. (The *Trib* didn't actually get around to sinking for a year or so after I left.) It wasn't a bad life. When the book came out, I was for a time there what my friends called "a famous arther"; I had received a small advance for a second novel from my publisher and had fallen in with a bad crowd of really amusing people who planned to be famous arthers, too.

Soon, much too soon, the once great old *Herald Tribune* finally did succumb to another newspaper strike, and it didn't take long for me to realize I needed a day job, since being a famous arther, while fun and in some ways satisfying on certain levels, didn't hardly pay anything at all.

So, I became a journalism professor at Texas Christian University in Fort Worth, and three years later, Acting Chairman of the Journalism Department at Southern Methodist University in Dallas. I would have preferred just being a famous arther for the rest of my days, but having only one novel under my belt and it being mainly writing Mississippi out of my system and leaving that time of my life behind me, I found I didn't really have any idea how to write a novel. The one I had written had come so easily I had learned very little about the mechanics of the craft. I found also that, while writing journalism all those years had taught me a great deal about crafting sentences and paragraphs and newspaper length features, that kind of writing could be (as I think Hemingway once pointed out) detrimental to creating literature, if done for too long.

My friend Billie Lee Brammer said approximately the same things about his lingering inability to finish his second novel.

"I wrote three short stories," Billie Lee told me. "I don't know how to write a novel."

The fact was, as most of his friends eventually came to understand along the way, Billie Lee could have written another novel, if he could have overcome his angst and his complexes, including the one with the prefix "inferiority." Then, too, there was the fact that he had created *The Gay Place* mostly on the night beat at the White House for *Time* magazine while under the influence of the "diet pill" Dexamil, and he was convinced he couldn't write another novel without taking Dexamil, or the equivalent. And the nature of these so-called "diet" pills was that the more one took, the more one needed to take to achieve the same wide-awake, energetic effect. So, Billie Lee soon reached the point where he had to have the pills just to stay awake. The periods of euphoric confidence, when they occurred at all, became too brief to maintain continuity of thought long enough to write a book.

How, you may ask, do I know about such things?

Because I, too, traveled that road. When I moved from TCU to SMU, I was not planning to make a career as an administrator. In the first place, I had a Master's Degree, but no doctorate. And in the second place, I had found during my years at TCU that I enjoyed teaching. I quickly discovered as acting chairman that teaching had to take a back seat to the paper shuffling necessary for a department administrator, all those meetings the chairman must attend, and the growing lines of students to advise and counsel regarding which courses to take or whether or not to major in journalism or switch to some other field—maybe education, which I learned during my teaching years was the major many matriculators (let's not call them students) who found they could not make it in other fields were counseled into. This was true on all three campuses where I taught, as well as the three universities where I was listed as a student so I could play on the varsity football teams. I assumed, therefore, it was true almost universally. This, perhaps, explains why so many of our public school teachers are such—well, have such limited educations themselves. Someday, we should all pray, our public schools will certify teachers by subject matter rather than the number of hours they have in "Education" and, in turn, pay them enough to attract the best college students rather than shuffling off with all the others who couldn't cut it in other fields. (Exceptions duly noted, please.)

That's a purely personal opinion, of course, and I detest exposing my convictions regarding teachers and teacher education. I loved teaching, and some of my favorite relatives were teachers, excellent ones, but they were educated before university Education Schools took over the training of our public school teachers.

Anyway, one of my jobs as Acting Chairman of the SMU Journalism Department was to search for the permanent Ph.D. chairman. My plan was to scour the nation to find an administrator type whose philosophy of Journalism and Journalism Education was the same as mine. Then I could concentrate on teaching a few courses I was good at because of my background, education and temperament. As Acting Chairman, with only Brammer teaching one course and Peter Gent teaching a night class in advertising, it had been necessary for me to teach four different classes each semester. That's eight distinct courses each school year—unheard of at a major university, and definitely not conducive to teaching excellence. Although I had my moments, from time to time, I'm a bit afraid they were not momentous moments. As a small department, most of my classes were filled with students who had me as an instructor in at least one other course and had, therefore, heard all my stories by the time they walked into one of my classes the second or third time, which made it hard to come up with new stuff as either teacher or entertainer—which all good teachers have to be at least to a degree.

I could hardly wait to find the perfect candidate for permanent chairman so I could teach the same classes more than once without having to invent them from scratch and without having to spend so much time shuffling papers. I finally discovered this young Ph.D. from Indiana, who agreed with me on everything. We relaxed in his hotel room one night and discussed Journalism Education from A to Z and we were in perfect harmony all the way. I was elated. Even when a couple of my best students, after meeting with this paragon, came by my office with their thumbs pointed downward, shaking their heads from side to side in a negative, no-way-José manner. They were only students. What did they know?

I had my life from that point on all mapped out: All the moving around I'd done as a working newspaperman and my natural tendency to believe I would live and be healthy forever had caused me to ignore the fact that someday I might not be able to work and draw wages. I never learned—because I don't think anyone ever told me—about such aspects of life as saving for one's old age, or even a time when the pay checks might not be coming in regularly. I'd always had a job, and I just naturally assumed I always would. In other words, I hadn't saved a dime for my future, and until I went to work at SMU, I never gave any real thought to such matters as that. But they had a pension fund at SMU, and something called "tenure" that assured certain professors of permanent job security—unless they screwed up royally, which I never intended to do.

I worked harder and longer hours at SMU than I'd ever worked before in my life, and my work produced better results than it ever had before. The word had gone out, spread mainly by a student named Don Brown, a campus leader who had dropped journalism as a major his sophomore year but came back onto the fold after a long discussion with me in my office. Brown would be editor of the campus newspaper his senior year. It wasn't long until Brown and most of the other journalism students were calling me by my first name and gathering in my office to discuss their various academic and personal triumphs and tribulations.

One who spent time in my office between classes was Max Woodfin, who during his senior year was named by Sigma Delta Chi, the professional journalism society, as the nation's top journalism student. Brown went to work for UPI after graduating, and Woodfin spent two years emptying bed pans at a hospital in Galveston to atone for being a pacifist during the Vietnam tragedy. Then, after working at a couple of pretty good daily newspapers, Woodfin moved to Austin, where he wrote speeches for the late, great Barbara Jordan.

I include this digression into my brief career as a departmental chairman at Southern Methodist University only to lead us up to the point of my breakdown.

Peter Gent had warned me. My situation wasn't as secure as I'd assumed. After an angry encounter with our fabulous new permanent chairman, Gent resigned his ad hoc teaching position that paid almost enough to buy the gas it took to get him to class each evening. He resigned because the new chairman made demands Pete considered arrogant and less than necessary, treated him as if he were teaching that course because he needed the job and not because he was doing it as a personal favor to me. Pete said to me, "Jay, if you think that (expletive deleted) is going to let you hang around to look over his shoulder, you're crazy."

I, of course, haw hawed him off, attributing the whole thing to Pete's righteous anger.

But the truth was, I had already begun to feel a nagging doubt in the back of my own mind. Yes, the new chairman and I had agreed completely during our relaxed discussions early on, but there were definitely warning signs that should have alerted me to the fact that the guy's philosophy of journalism education was not exactly carved in stone.

I had talked with editors on the East Coast—the *Washington Post, Boston Globe* and others—and found they had no respect for the standard journalism curriculum. "We can teach a kid to write a news story," one managing editor told me, and his peers agreed, "but we can't educate them and we can't teach them how to write good basic sentences and paragraphs."

That made perfect sense to me, and I had taken the concept as gospel and geared my curriculum that first year, when I was both chairman and faculty, toward meeting those needs. I advised my aspiring journalists to take a minimum of journalism courses and declare double majors—in journalism and, say, political science, or history, or if they wanted to specialize, in some field such as drama, or business or science. This theory motivated our majors to take nearly half their courses in other departments and schools, which I learned later, did not delight my dean.

And the new department chairman, despite our long conversation in the hotel that famous evening, chose, without a moment's hesitation, to agree with the dean, who expressed his fervent desire to enroll as many students as possible in as many journalism courses as possible. I learned later that the school had a special arrangement set up with SMU whereby the Dean got $50 a head for every student taking a course in his school, which was, by the way, the School of Fine Arts, and included broadcasting and film.

Years later, after much more water had flowed beneath many of my bridges, I listened to my friend Joe Murray give a piece of advice to a grumbling managing editor who had just lost an argument with his publisher and declared staunchly: "You have to admit I'm right."

"No, I don't," Joe told him. "The reason I don't is the boss is always right unless you can convince him he's wrong."

It struck me that this was a rule I had never learned, and it probably had cost me plenty over the years, even though I sometimes declared, not entirely without pride: "I never gave a damn inch."

So, the new department chairman and the dean of the School of Fine Arts at Southern Methodist University disagreed with my philosophy of journalism education and I never gave a damn inch. Guess who stayed and guess who left.

Incidentally, or maybe not so incidentally, at about the time of the debacle at SMU, my wife and I were breaking up. Broke up, in point of fact, and so my young daughter and I moved to Fort Worth where I spent almost a year as a Public Broadcasting newsman at Channel 13. A year, I must admit, I've almost no recollection of living and working. The SMU job had been my Plan A, and I had no Plan B, and I was forty-eight years old. When you are nearing fifty and have no Plan B, Depression with a capital D can move in with little or no resistance, and set up housekeeping in your brain.

About all I do remember about that year with PBS's Channel 13 in Dallas and my part in the "Newsroom," the program that had been so successful under the guidance of Jim Lehrer before he left for a similar project in Washington, D.C., is that it takes about one minute to read one page, double-spaced—which means TV news segments that last two minutes—and it must be earth-shakingly important to be allowed a full two minutes of air time—are about two double-spaced pages long. Compared to the same story for a newspaper that would be maybe as long as four to six pages. I have never forgotten this bit of trivia because it made an deep impression, even upon my fevered brain, that television news programs must squeeze their most important stories of the day into one or two, doubled-spaced, typed pages. Yet, according to what we are told, most Americans get all of their news from television. Small wonder so many people know so little about what's really going on in this country and in the world—not to mention their own cities, counties and states—in the so-called Information Age.

I don't think I was a very good TV news person. No one ever came right out and said so, but the other thing about that job I remember is that I couldn't for the life of me speak without reading my copy, word-for-word, right off the page. Others seemed to only glance at their copy sheets occasionally, while my eyes were always locked on the pages on the table in front of me.

My mental processes were warped that year, not only by the persistent Depression with a capital D, but by amphetamine pills I was swallowing like baby aspirin all day to be able to face the world. Just to be able to get out of bed each day and get a little work done.

So, there I was—on the boob tube almost every evening, stammering and halting and pausing in all the wrong places and trying, as often as not unsuccessfully, to squeeze the essence of a news story into one double-spaced page. I was pretty good on feature stories, I think, and that was mainly because the Dallas PBS affiliate at that time had some excellent kind-hearted filmmakers on staff who kept me from making a complete ass of myself. I had done three highly praised features before I found out you were supposed to write a rough script, or at least some kind of outline, before the photographer did his work, giving him something to go by. What a concept.

So you see what I mean about how kind the station's cinematographers were to me. They went right ahead shooting their film first, never complaining or calling me a fool, then I would look at their rough film and write my scripts. I'll be forever grateful.

Ironically, during the year I was barely escaping total humiliation on TV on almost every weekday evening, people I had known for years would go out of their way to stop me on the street, or in a supermarket, to rave about how happy they were I had finally made it Big. I stifled my desire to yell back at my "fans" that in my opinion, being on a local PBS TV show was probably the least important I had ever done as an adult. Why is it that when people see you on television they are impressed beyond all reason?

Meantime, I was offered teaching jobs at Marquette University in Milwaukee and Wichita State University in Wichita, Kansas. But after seriously considering both offers, I decided to stay in Texas—regardless of what the future here might hold for me. I felt I had roamed around too much in my adult life already and ought to stay put for awhile and see what happened. Whether or not this decision was reached from some innate wisdom or as a result of my zombie-like condition I still can't say for sure. But I stayed in Texas.

When my career as a TV star was obviously going nowhere, I resigned and took over as editor of *Iconoclast*, a weekly that its young publisher, Doug Baker, claimed to want to turn into a legitimate publication, one that would have respect in the community—at least a considerable part of the community, since we're talking about Dallas in the 1970s here. I accepted that challenge because I had nothing better to do at the time and was still half crazy anyhow.

In a kind of circuitous way, *Iconoclast* had evolved from what had been Dallas's underground newspaper in the sixties, when underground newspapers were all the rage on college campuses. In its original form, it was called *Notes from the Underground* (or simply *Notes*) and was put out by SMU students. This was before I went to SMU, so I'm not familiar, first-hand, with exactly what went on then, but I've heard that a couple of the original student publishers of *Notes* were kicked out of school, or resigned just ahead of dismissal.

I severed relations with *Iconoclast* publisher Doug Baker not long after I met Willie Nelson and started writing about him and other principals of the Texas music uprising and, eventually, doing the programs for Willie's annual July 4th Picnics that drew thousands of fun-loving music lovers out into the scorching July Texas sun for annual country music versions of Woodstock. That life had its interesting moments, but I had this deeply ingrained habit, left over from my years on afternoon newspapers, of waking up early every morning regardless of how late I had stayed up the night before and not being able to sleep in the day time. That habit, plus the pills I took to keep me moving and awake at night, not to mention the continuing, persistent state of Depression, a condition that seemed to worsen in the company of those musicians who were doing their thing with originality and skill, while I felt more and more, deep down in my soul, that I was turning into nothing more than a groupie, all of this piling up finally broke me completely down, and for the first time since I was fourteen years old, I went home to Mama to have a place to lie down long enough to figure out where I had been and where I ought to be going.

So, I'd been sleeping off and on at Mama's nearly all day every day for about two weeks and thought I felt better than I really did when I got the call from Roy Stamps saying he'd talked to Willie and they'd decided to put on a concert "to raise money, so Jay can put out a magazine about Texas music." I told Roy I didn't feel up to putting out a magazine, but he kept talking and I finally said, "Okay, if Willie wants me to, I'll do it."

They had the concert in the SMU gym. When word went around that Willie was going to do it, other Texas picker poets were eager to jump in, too. Jerry Jeff Walker volunteered. ("See how much everybody loves you," said his wife, Susan.) Steve Fromholz said he'd be the master of ceremonies. Guy Clark heard about it and volunteered to perform. Rusty Weir showed up with his band. And Bonnie Bramlet walked on stage that night from somewhere and sang a couple of songs with Willie. So did Spanky of Spanky and Our Gang.

The *Texas Music Magazine* Concert was a big success, to say the least. The initial bank deposit was something over sixty thousand dollars. I knew it wouldn't be easy to start up a slick magazine with that little bit of money, but I figured I could do it with a little help from my friends.

It was the last thing I wanted to do, or should have resorted to, but since I wound up having to do the editorial part of *Texas Music* without a staff, I rounded up a supply of what Billie Lee Brammer called "heart medicine" and went to work.

Zip ah dee do dah, zip ah de ay, my oh my, what a wonderful day . . .

WheRE Do OLd MAdDOgS Go?

The Rise and Fall of an Expert Listener

The magazine, *Texas Music*, was both a success and a failure. Reactions from readers, all the way from the West Coast, were almost a hundred percent favorable. Ads came pouring in, sometimes without even being solicited. Subscriptions came in in remarkable numbers, considering the fact we did no advertising or other promotions. It was an almost totally word-of-mouth deal, although that certainly wasn't the way it should have been.

I got a call one day from the noted record producer Bob Johnston, who is the "Bob" of Bob Dylan's famous question, "Is it rolling, Bob?" on Dylan's *Nashville Skyline* album. Johnston produced Billy Joe Shaver's second album, *When I Get My Wings*, that was backed by the distinctive rock guitar of Dickie Betts of the Alman Brothers Band, a far cry from Shaver's first album, *Old Five and Dimers*, which had garnered Billy Joe a network of cult followers across the country. The drastic change in both style and content of Shaver's second album caused many of his hard-core fans, as well as reviewers, to criticize both Billy Joe and his producer. What seemed to bother some Shaver freaks, it seemed, was Betts's guitar contributions. He had chosen to back Shaver's raw, rhythmic vocals with an exquisitely liquid sound that floats incredibly close to Billy Joe's pitch. I admitted in my review this was a little disturbing to me the first time I listened to the album, but the more I heard it, the better I liked it and became convinced it was the most creative way possible to support Shaver's singing and lyrics, which were—are—even farther out than the lyrics of his first album, which is saying something.

Anyhow . . .

I got this call from Bob Johnston in San Francisco, bragging on me for being what he called "the only reviewer so far," who understood what he and Shaver and Betts were doing on the album. Johnston told me he had picked up a copy of *Texas Music* on the airplane flying back to San Francisco and just happened to see the review, and he wanted to subscribe. For some strange reason, our subscriptions from California outnumbered those from Texas.

So, the future looked bright there for awhile for the brand new *Texas Music* magazine.

Until the checks started bouncing.

Big checks, little checks and middle-sized checks. Checks for $100, the token payment I made to some first-rate magazine writers who agreed to write for that paltry amount to help us get started. This, dear reader, was extremely embarrassing, especially since these were professional friends of mine. So, I went to our bank to check on the magazine's balance, just two issues and two months after the debut edition and the famous fund-raising concert.

Balance: Zero.

Right then is when I should have had a showdown with our supposedly temporary publisher, but since I had no editorial staff—I was writing or rewriting almost every article, using pen names such as M. D. Shafter and putting only my initials at the end of an article—and at the same time, taking ads over the telephone, conferring with our graphics man, Buffalo George Toomer, editing copy, throughout every day and far into the nights—and so on and on—I put it off.

That's my excuse and I'm sticking to it.

The truth is, or was . . . well, the truth is and was I intuitively knew exactly what was going on and couldn't face up to the reality of it. Facing up to it would have meant taking legal action. By the time the situation had disintegrated to that point, I was discouraged by Willie, who was inherently against such things as taking people to court for—in effect—stealing. If Willie hadn't been firmly against that sort of thing, he undoubtedly would have sued a lot of hangers-on over the years.

Once, during an interview with Willie for his book, *The Incredible Rise of Redneck Rock,* Jan Reid noted, after a series of anecdotes about Willie's "Forty Thieves" and how they had managed in various hilariously transparent ways to profit from their association with Nelson, Jan asked Willie why he didn't get rid of those people, get them off his back and stop them from literally swindling him and his organization. Willie's answer was wonderful, authentic Willie: "Those guys have families to support, too."

So, anyhow, nothing got done about the magazine's dire fiscal predicament, and I continued to avoid thinking about it and continued my correspondence with the man I hoped would come to Dallas to take over as publisher—Hank Poirot, an Amarillo native who was working on a national magazine out of San Francisco and was interested in getting back to Texas. Hank knew Willie and was a fan of the Texas music uprising already. He thought the concept of *Texas Music* was a great idea, and when the time was right for him to get away from his San Francisco base, he flew to Dallas to look into our enterprise more closely.

Meantime, Steve Murrin, a colorful Fort Worth entrepreneur who had this dream of developing the old Fort Worth stockyards area into a realistic wild west tourist and historic attraction, invited me and the magazine to move into an office in the Cowtown Coliseum he would provide free, hoping that having us there would attract the picker poets and their fans to hang out there and add to the area's cowboy ambiance. By that time, I had taken issue number four of the magazine to the printer and had learned, when we called to find out if the copies were ready for us to pick up, that the check for the printing had bounced like an NBA basketball. The printer was furious and vowed to burn every copy of that edition in his possession if we didn't come up with the cash muy pronto.

Hank and Steve Murrin's accountant managed to sweet talk the justifiably irate printer into letting them have a few copies of that historic final edition, and it might have been the best one yet. It had blues belter Tracy Nelson (no relation to Willie or, as far as I know, to the actress of the same name) on the cover and a pretty good interview with her inside with my own byline on it. Too bad the public never got to read it and see the accompanying photos and other articles. Those few copies, if they still exist somewhere, no doubt will be valuable collector's items, because issue number four never came out.

Maybe the most ironic angle of the sudden demise of *Texas Music* was the fact that *Playboy* and the Southland Corporation (with its chain of 7-11 stores) were showing interest in buying outright or investing in the project. I was rapidly running out of steam, and planned to peddle it to one of those outfits, appoint myself a younger, less worn out, editor and step aside to become something of a consultant.

But Hank Poirot and the accountant were able to dig up enough of the financial details to discover that Mr. Temporary Publisher had borrowed money in the magazine's name from at least two Dallas banks and were, therefore, afraid to associate themselves with a publication in such shaky fiscal circumstances, for fear that the facts they were able to unearth in only a few days were just the tip of an even bigger iceberg, and that Mr. Publisher might well have gone into hock in the name of *Texas Music* to no telling how many other lending institutions and gullible individuals.

Bless their hearts, Jerry Jeff and Willie both, at separate times, volunteered to hold another concert to raise more money to "save the magazine." By that time, however, I was so embarrassed that I had allowed the situation to get that far out of hand mainly because I had been too exhausted to face what I intuitively knew was happening behind my back that I said, "Thanks, but never mind."

I had spent almost an entire year on this project and used up just about every dime and ounce of energy I had. But, looking back on that year, I find lots of things to laugh about. As they say: "Someday we'll look back at this and laugh." And so we have.

For instance, the original deal was to spread the *Texas Music* stock among several of us, including Willie, Jerry Jeff, Bud Shrake (for writing an article for the debut edition) and, of course, myself. For months, I periodically asked our "temporary" publisher for the stock certificates and the official papers that go along with forming a corporation, so I could bestow them upon the other stockholders (and hold one in my own hands, as well). He kept putting me off with stories about how the lawyers were procrastinating, and I don't remember what all. Finally, when the whole thing fell in on itself, and there was nothing there but a tall stack of unpaid bills, we found out Mr. Temporary Publisher had never actually gotten around to doing any of those things one does when a new corporation starts up. There were no articles of incorporation, no official books, no organizational minutes, no assignments of ownership of the magazine to anyone but himself and a mysterious partner whose name or connection I never learned before I fled the scene of the crime.

There is always the possibility that the Temporary Publisher kept the magazine all to himself out of the goodness of his heart to protect the other principals—or maybe he just outsmarted himself.

● ● ●

Yes, there are times in one's life, if one has ventured out there far enough, when one reaches the point where he is prepared to beg. There've been times when I was at that point. The period immediately following the *Texas Music* fiasco was one of them. Friends, I went so far as to start buttering up the bastards to set the stage for a full scale surrender. The man who never gave a damn inch was ready to beg for a job. There are different kinds of supplication, of course, but it's all begging.

Once before, when I was much younger, I had gone to our nation's capital to surrender, figuring that was the place to do it. But all I learned there is that Washington women were all divorcees with one and a half children and that when you walked into their apartments, they immediately played Barbra Streisand's "People, people who need people, are the *something something* people in the world."

I didn't surrender there and then because—well, because that music was too corny to surrender to, or some damn thing.

Anyway, I kind of got a second wind and came up with an idea and wound up going back to Texas and teaching Journalism.

This time, after the magazine had wrung what little juice was left out of me, I wound up in Lufkin, where I got fat and was saved, not necessarily in that order.

The Best Years?

My high school coach, Goober Keyes, used to tell us we would look back on those times as the best years of our lives, and I believed him. I assumed I would always live in Lubbock, and wanted to very much because I was sure Lubbock was the ideal place to live. It was just the right size—about thirty or forty thousand folks who looked suspiciously at the world in the New Mexico mountains we sometimes swore we could see when we looked across the high flat plains to the west, and down off the Caprock to the east where, when you got through the red clay gullies of big ranches, there was only Fort Worth and Dallas, and who wanted to live in those huge cities? Lubbock was a college town. Texas Tech served as the border on the west side of town. There was only one high school, as far as we were concerned. I still don't know where the few black and Hispanic kids attended classes. If, indeed, they did.

Everybody knew just about everybody else and there seemed (in my mind anyhow) no class distinctions beyond that of color, which was an invisible flaw to me then, as it was to probably most of my friends. The only black people I can recall seeing in Lubbock were two who worked for one of the town's wealthiest families, who had a daughter my age and a younger son, so I visited their mansion now and then. This was during the Great Depression and being poor was not uncommon. You were accepted by one of the two or three "In" groups in high school, not because of the way you dressed, or the car you drove or the material possessions you managed to accumulate, but because you were gifted in some field, were particularly likable, really funny or smart, or a combination of two or more of the above.

There have been times in my life when I was convinced Coach Goober was right about those high school years being the best of all, but there were other times I was sure my friend Gary Cartwright's high school coach knew more about the real world.

"Before each game, he'd tell us, 'It's dog-eat-dog out there, boys,'" Cartwright told me. "I thought he was saying 'doggydog,' and wondered what he meant."

Thinking more on the subject, however, I've decided Coach Goober and Cartwright's coach were saying approximately the same thing. But in the years since high school, despite the fact that I loved those years when I was living them, I've come to realize they were a long way from being my best.

It would be hard to pick The Best Years of My Life, because my best times came in shorter segments than years. They came in moments, days and nights, and, a few times back there, whole weeks, and even a couple of Best Months. In other words, I've been to the mountain a few times, but never managed to stay up there so long I got used to it. My few years as a Famous Arther had their moments, but weren't what one could accurately label as "Wonderful," because my private life was such a mess, I spent a lot of time and chemicals hiding from it.

I now believe my high school years were blissful because teenagers generally were as ignorant as house pets. I say "were" because kids these days apparently aren't as protected from the doggy-dog outside world as we were in my pre-WWII teen years. And that's too bad. For them, not us.

Rather, I should say, there is such a thing as believing too soon that you are grown up. I used to raise cane at parents (as an editorial writer for a small daily) for allowing—for encouraging, as was most often the case—their kids to have elementary school graduation ceremonies and junior high proms. Once the kids have been through all those teen rituals as preteens, there's no glitter left for the real thing when it comes along in the customary course of events. So the kids must move on to other means of getting the kicks that once were allotted for proms and graduation festivities and accompanying frivolities. That's why kids are drinking and doing drugs at younger and younger ages. At least, I'm convinced that's one of the big reasons. By the time they are in college, occasionally getting slightly tipsy is no longer a fascinating or provocative ritual of youthful derring-do, so they drink to get as drunk as possible, and do other dangerously stupid things for rebellious thrills.

If this sounds oversimplified, think about it again (to paraphrase Faulkner, who used to tell his critics who said they didn't understand his last book: "Read it again.")

So, anyhow—I wound up living in Lubbock less than a full year as an adult, despite my teenage vows to always live there, and my high school years weren't my best any way you evaluate them. Nevertheless, I still consider my teenage years as an excellent time. I was a happy kid. My junior high dreams of making the varsity starting line up at Lubbock High came true when I was a junior. And my sophomore year I got to go along with the famous Cinderella Kids as they won their way to the state championship game in the Cotton Bowl in Dallas a few days before Christmas in 1939. I even got to play a few minutes in those championship games, including the final triumph in the Cotton Bowl. But they weren't my best years. My instincts somehow told me I didn't know a whole lot when it came right down to it. About anything, really, except maybe football.

I sure didn't know anything useful about girls, and that caused me some anxiety and bewilderment from time to time. A great deal of both, in point of fact. I still don't know much about them, but I have learned, over the years and from my many mistakes in that area, not to be so uptight about it. My fairly new attitude toward the opposite sex is summed in that song Doris Day sang in that old movie: "Kay say-ra say-ra." After all, Sigmund Freud's last words on his deathbed were supposed to have been: "What do women want?" I've learned to answer: "Whatever will be will be."

I'm just grateful to Fate, or whatever powers there may be, that I was, at last, fortunate enough to join hands and hearts with a woman who, strange as some of her ways may be, is my soulmate on the really vital aspects of life and living and being together. She's had as much difficulty getting here as I have. Maybe that's why we are so tolerant toward each other's quirks and eccentricities, which are miraculously alike.

But I'm getting ahead of myself.

I'm not sure even now how I feel, what I believe, about Destiny and Guardian Angels and stuff like that, but when I think back over how I got to Lufkin it almost makes me pretty sure that something along that line may influence our lives; not control, but influence. It's too much for me to swallow whole that there is something or someone out there actually controlling every move we make. In my mind, that's not how it works. I don't know how or why, but something got me to Lufkin when it wasn't even logical, much less anticipated.

The way it happened was unusual enough on the face of it, since my mother was never one to make impulsive decisions even about minor things, and certainly not about really significant matters, such as selling her house in Fort Worth and moving to a whole other town, something she hadn't done in more than thirty years. She was a cautious woman. Always had been. If a rain came along at the end of a long drought, her first verbalized thought was always something on the order of: "I hope we don't have a flood and get washed away."

But a few months after my daughter Carter and I moved into mother's house in Fort Worth, just after the untimely demise of *Texas Music Magazine* and my collapse, she returned from a visit to her sister in the Deep East Texas town where she was born and grew to be a teenager, but hadn't been back, except to visit kinfolks, in more than fifty years. This house, she announced, was laid out perfectly for the three of us, and Carter, who had just graduated from high school, could attend Stephen F. Austin University, a mere twenty-minute drive from our new domicile.

My reaction was something along the lines of, "Cool. Wake me up when it's time to move." Little did I know that my life was about to undergo some major changes from that day forward.

I didn't quit cold turkey. The first months—actually, the first few years—I lived in Lufkin, I maintained contact with Austin friends, but it was mostly by phone. Susan Streit Walker and Cookie DeShay, with whom I had shared a house in Austin for a short while in 1974 when I was working on that year's Willie Nelson July 4th Picnic, kept me in touch. Susan and Jerry Jeff were married in 1974, and after I moved to Lufkin, she called about once a month and told me who was doing what and urged me to visit them in their home just west of Austin. I spent a Thanksgiving there. One year, a Lufkin friend, Rick Pezdirtz, was chairman of the Lufkin community concert series and we invited Jerry Jeff to do his single act as one of the series attractions. They sold a bunch of tickets to people who'd never been to a community concert before and confused some of the regular members, but all in all, it was a success.

Meantime, I had started hanging out with Joe Murray, who taught me such valuable things as to how to chitchat and got me started writing a weekly column for the *Lufkin Daily News* and the Cox newspaper chain, which I did for more than fifteen years.

Recovering
in Lufkin

One day, about the middle of the 1980s, Homer and I were standing in his South Austin kitchen talking about the Good Old Days. Homer's blond-red beard was streaked with gray now and he wasn't as skinny as he used to be.

Homer had lived in Austin, more or less, since he got out of the service, having been a lieutenant in Vietnam. When he finally got back home he decided the best policy for the rest of his life would be to think good thoughts and make himself as invisible as possible in today's computerized society. Homer supported his various hobbies, such as eating and playing harmonica, by hiring out as a cabinet maker and carpenter. He played harmonica well enough to sit in with some of Austin's better groups during the Texas music uprising, particularly bands supporting Jerry Jeff Walker, Billy Joe Shaver, Steve Fromholz, et al.

As a matter of fact, those were the Good Old Days Homer and I were remembering—the early and middle years of the seventies. Together, we lamented that country music was back in the hands of the Nashville moguls. That distinctive uniqueness of Texas music—labeled by Fromholz as "folk, rock, jazz, country, blues, pop"—or something like that—had been incorporated into the syrupy Nashville Sound, and the hunky men and women now selling most of the records resemble models for western wear catalogues, unlike the grungy musicians who lived on the road, the way Willie and Jerry Jeff, Ray Wylie Hubbard, Billy Joe Shaver and other Texas picker poets did. That's what happens, of course. Like the pop standards of the thirties and forties, good music never dies, it just moves to Nashville and adds a steel guitar.

Willie had become a national icon—like ice cream and Bing Crosby. Jerry Jeff had astounded everybody who knew him by turning into the best husband and father of the bunch. Shrake and Cartwright were making movies with Willie Nelson and Kris Kristofferson, who had sort of joined the Texas bunch on a sometimes basis. Guy Clark was in Nashville becoming the dean of Nashville songwriters. Nearly all the Maddogs, both singing and otherwise, had been noticeably slowed down by Mother Nature—time and mileage proving they were not bullet-proof after all. Dan Jenkins's books were selling so well he was the zillionaire elder statesman. But then he always had been, in a way.

Jerry Jeff's wife Susan was now his manager, and they were doing better than ever, and hanging onto Jerry Jeff's inimitable personal style by putting out their own records. The big record companies, Jerry Jeff had told me, "want to pick my songs and session musicians and everything else that would wipe out everything we've been working for, as far as having control over the music is concerned."

"It's getting so you can't sit in with anybody anymore," Homer complained. "Everybody's got arrangements now. Even Fromholz has arrangements, for crying out loud."

The prime driving force of the Texas music uprising of the seventies—as it usually is in "outlaw" movements in the arts—

was the desire of musicians to play their music the way they felt it should be played, free of the dictates of professional organizers and record company pencil pushers. When the cohesive audience for their music grew older and started staying home more and more, and as a new, younger audience gradually took their place, the whole scene changed.

"I'll tell you when it started going downhill," Homer declared. "It started going downhill when they changed that law where clubs don't have to close until 2 A.M. That's when it started going downhill. When the clubs shut down at midnight, everybody was still revved up and ready to pick some more and we'd go to somebody's house or motel room. Since they started staying open 'til 2 A.M., everybody's too tired or drunk, or both, to start any serious picking again. So they go home and go to bed. Or look for women and nobody gets together trading licks anymore."

I had turned away to replenish my apple juice and, when I turned back, Homer was nowhere to be seen. He had been standing in a corner with no windows or doors—and now he was gone.

● ● ●

But the eighties hadn't been all bad for everybody. My own head was clearing up as I assessed my strengths and, especially, my weaknesses. When Homer disappeared through that windowless, doorless wall, I headed for home. In those days, home was Lufkin, deep in East Texas—where I was living with my mother. I told my Austin friends who asked, and all of them had in one way or another, that I had made the move because I couldn't afford Betty Ford's place. That's not exactly the whole story, but it was symbolically truthful.

In Lufkin, I found the time and space to contemplate my navel, because nobody I knew ever drove through there on purpose. Being a person of fairly weak will, I reasoned, I would be less tempted to backslide there by myself, with my mother close at hand to wait on me until I grew stronger physically and emotionally. It was the first time I had lived with the strong, quiet woman who had given birth to me since I was fourteen—more than forty years before. More than anything else, I needed a safe place to rest my aching head for awhile. Soon, I was getting plenty of sleep and walking great distances every morning. In Lufkin I met a young man who would become the finest friend of my life, something a bit unusual for a man my age. And, after almost two decades, I was able to write something longer than magazine and newspaper pieces.

My new best friend was Joe Murray, who, like me, had old-fashioned ideas about a newspaper's place in the community, and was in a position to implement them as editor and publisher of the *Lufkin Daily News*. Ironically enough, Joe was an ardent fan of several of my writer friends—McMurtry, Brammer, Cartwright, King and Willie. My tall tales about his heroes—and I had a few (some of them true)—intrigued Joe, both as a fan and as a storyteller himself of some note in the Piney Woods where his columns were avidly read even before they were syndicated by Cox Newspapers and distributed all around the country. Not long before I met Joe, he and Ken Herman, one of his reporters, were awarded a Pulitzer Prize for community service.

In Lufkin, I even started writing a new novel, in which I transferred some of my own dark contemplations into a character I called Wally Banner, who might have been modeled after Billie Lee Brammer. Recently, looking back over the pages in that novel (as yet unpublished because I couldn't face the task of rewriting it a third time without threatening to puke), I found sections that were eerily self revealing. For example, this stream of consciousness segment:

... He was afraid to contemplate his future and the prospect of reflecting on the past was horrendous. With his yesterdays and tomorrows unthinkable, he managed to sustain himself in the Now any way he could, chemicals and sex being his best bets thus far. He wanted to believe in himself again, and in someone else again, somewhere deep inside himself he wanted this, but he shied away from both because he feared his heart and ego could not endure being ripped asunder one more time. It might drive him over the edge. He was sure it would as often as he was sure it wouldn't. He was an emotional coward and no longer bothered to deny it. Better to be a reasonably functional coward than a mad man. This was his ongoing philosophy of day-to-day living, which made it progressively harder for him to draw conclusions and apparently impossible for him to finish anything he started. He had tried, several times, to let go, to slip on down into madness, figuring he would then at least be cared for and no longer pushed. (Didn't some tribes revere the village idiot?) But he had not been able to let go, perhaps because that, too, required making a decision, choosing a definite course of action and following through. No, he clung to his sanity like an exhausted mountain climber clinging to a crumbling crevice in the rock, fingers bleeding but still hanging on.

Reading this piece of writing long after it was written and realizing it was as much about myself as it was about Billie

Lee, was a little frightening. By the time I wrote that passage, I was well past the point of hanging on by bloody fingernails, but just the idea, the realization that I actually had been there, was troublesome. Just to realize I had once been at that precarious point in my life—renewed my resolve to continue working my way back to being the person I knew I had been before I started trying to be the character certain others believed I was.

Besides being a little frightening, it was disturbingly fascinating to finally be able to face the image of myself others had in their minds and to be able to accept the fact that their image had greatly influenced the person I had gradually turned into since my return to Texas. Not that the person I had become was basically terrible, but that man is not the person I really was, or wanted to be, when I thought on it seriously, and with a clear head. It made me wonder how many others out there had become someone other than their real, deep-down selves just because their friends and associates had, for one reason or other, developed images of them beyond their true selves and they had tried to live up to those images. Image may not be everything, as the man on TV claimed, but it is a force to be reckoned with.

In my semi-isolation in deep East Texas, I was attempting to simplify my life, hone my daily objectives and long-term goals down to one or two, utilize my time better, learn not to be scattered in my thoughts and actions—to get back to the old me. When people called and invited me to join them in this or that endeavor—even something as non-threatening as serving on the local library board—I learned to say no. Politely. Thanks, but no thanks. I'm trying to simplify my life.

One of the advantages of my friendship with Joe Murray was learning to chitchat. To those who have always been able to chitchat, this may seem trivial. But not to me. I'm not certain I understand why I was never an accomplished chitchatter, but I wasn't, and this deficiency bothered me for years. This reminds me of the night when Billy Joe Shaver told me with his characteristic directness: "Sometimes I stay away from you, Jay, because we always get into such serious conversations and I'm not always ready for that." At the time I didn't know whether to take Billy Joe's remark as a compliment or as an insult. I still don't. But, knowing Billy Joe—or I should say, having known him back in those days—I'm inclined to believe he didn't mean it either way. Billy Joe usually just said whatever he was thinking at the moment, with no hidden agenda or meaning behind his words. I could never be sure he wasn't putting me on with his "country" talk and mannerisms one minute and his near-genius brilliance the next.

But—this part is supposed to be about my friend Joe Murray and his part in my Lufkin recovery. Joe taught me how to chitchat at least partially by convincing me, in a number of ways, that I could trust him, that he would still be my friend—even if I said something silly or stupid from time to time. Always before, when I called anyone on the telephone, it was for a specific reason—to relay information or to ask a question. Never just to talk. Sometime along in there, after I realized Joe and I had become chitchatting buddies, both on the phone and in person, I figured out the reason I had never learned to be comfortable making small talk was probably because of those years as an adolescent in Lubbock when I never wanted to appear foolish or stupid or otherwise unworthy. That idea was buried deep in my consciousness for years.

There were times, even back in high school, when knowing how to chitchat might have made life easier for me. One of those times was the summer I worked for the telephone company teaching Lubbock residents how to use their brand new dial phones. At the week-long "school" to teach me and other members of the crew how to communicate our new-found knowledge about dialing phones, we were instructed to make telephone customers feel warm toward the phone company rather than angry because the system had been changed on them. To make sure we spent enough time with each customer, we were told to see no more than ten each day. Our days began at 8 A.M. and lasted until 5 P.M., with an hour off for lunch. That meant, if we did it the way we were told to do it, we would see five customers in the morning and five in the afternoon.

I always found I had seen all ten customers before noon. That was because, I now realize, I couldn't chitchat. I just walked into each house, told them who I was and why I was there and proceeded to teach them how to put their fingers in the little holes with the numbers in them and dial. I couldn't think of any chitchat to go along with that, and in just a few minutes, I would find myself out the door and on my way to the next house.

So the problem was: What could I do the rest of the day, the entire afternoon, that wouldn't expose myself as an incompetent chitchatter? The only thing I could think of was to find the nearest city park (Lubbock had city parks every few blocks in most residential areas in those days—pretty, green, well-kept city parks) and crawl under a shrub and sleep. So, that's what I did, almost every day. It was one of the best jobs I ever had. But it made me very nervous, hiding out like that. I almost had an ulcer by the end of the summer.

I don't mean to imply that Joe taught me "phony" chit-chat. He taught me how to swap trivial talk and enjoy it. There's a big difference. Joe would invite several friends out to his lake house, not far from town, but in the deep woods so it felt like you had been transported far from civilization—to eat barbecued chicken, or grilled steaks, maybe drink a little beer and tell tall tales. In other words: serious chitchatting sessions. Sometimes we gathered at the Lufkin home of our Congressman—Good Time Charlie Wilson. The usual suspects in attendance at Joe's lake place and Charlie's bachelor digs included Joe's brother, Ernest, also a newspaperman of some note who for awhile there worked for Charlie before the Congressman retired undefeated. Rick Pezdirtz, who played the stock market and bet on sporting events for a living (and seemed to do quite well) was usually there. And Glenn McCutchen, who came in from Atlanta to be editor and publisher of the Nacogdoches daily and moved later to publisher of the Lufkin daily after Joe was promoted to Senior Writer for Cox Newspapers. And last, but perhaps most important of all, Joe's Cousin Booger, the one he made famous in his columns. Booger was the only one of us who knew all about deep East Texas lore and the best way to barbecue critters. This was the basic group, although others joined us from time to time, primarily Phil Latham, who followed Joe as editor of the *Lufkin Daily News,* and Heber Taylor, who was managing editor of the Galveston daily last I heard.

I call our conversations serious chitchat, and that's right. But that wasn't all we did when we got together—all being serious observers of the human condition and such American phenomena as politics in a free-market society. We also, quite naturally—being well-rounded, well-read men of the world—offered our considered opinions of current movies, books, pop and country music and local and international gossip. Joe's brother Ernest, several years younger than the rest of us (particularly me, since I was at least a decade older than the other regulars), sometimes seemed to be intently observing and listening to the wisdom flowing from our mouths. It reminded me of how Brammer used to appear to observe and listen to those frolicking about where he sat. Every now and then Ernest, like Billie Lee, would offer some startlingly pertinent commentary on what he had just seen and heard.

I recall one evening—I think we were gathered on that particular occasion on the deck behind the Honorable Good Time Charlie Wilson's house overlooking a creek and Congressman Wilson's numerous provisions for squirrels, badgers, birds of various colors, and other varmints so plentiful in and around the town of Lufkin—when Ernest commented that perhaps we should form a group to go on TV, in the manner of one of the Sunday discussion shows (like the McLaughlin Group, David Brinkley's group and so on) and comment on politics, critique books, movies and music. Ernest's suggestion came following a contribution to the chitchat by someone (I think it was Pezdirtz) telling a long joke, and then forgetting the punch line. Just before that, someone else (I think it was Joe) had recommended that we see a current movie starring as he put it, "You know, that short guy with the hair who's really funny sometimes, but also can play serious parts. I forget the name of the movie, but it's really a good one. You all ought to go see it." Ernest suggested we name our show "The Alzheimer's Group," and it could be taped live at the "Lost in the 50s Roadhouse" or right there on Charlie Wilson's deck, or out at Joe's lake house. We all agreed that this was a first-rate idea and vowed to follow up on it one day soon. That was several years ago. I forget exactly how many. We'll get around to it one of these days, I'm confident.

Those gatherings in Lufkin and the trips by car I took with Joe to Florida and Washington, D. C. (taking a week driving up, a week driving back and spending a week there), besides being enjoyable and informative jaunts, caused me to gain a lot of extra poundage and taught me a number of positive things about male bonding. I'd always managed to have an adequate number of male friends, but I'd never before gotten as close to them as I had to some of my female friends. I don't mean romantic closeness—just solid friendship. I attributed this to the fact that I was never close to my father, but had always been very close to my mother. Growing up, I never had any hands-on training about how men were supposed to act on the job and in the company of their male peers. I never developed an interest in hunting or fishing or golfing, or any other grown-up male avocations and pastimes. My mental and emotional attitudes in this area are not easy to describe or explain. I simply had never been as relaxed and at ease around other men as I often was with my female friends. It was puzzling to me how so many men seemed to believe that females were inferior to the entire male gender. Maybe that's because my mother, a country girl—with little education but a great deal of pride and courage—did more for me and my siblings than any man.

I realize these may not be the admissions of a really macho kind of guy, but then, I've never seen myself as being a macho kind of guy. Never felt any need for it, in point of fact. I like to believe this is because I've never felt my manhood seriously threatened. I've had my share of insecure moments from time to time in my life, man and boy—about a number of things. Some of them silly, perhaps, and some not. But never about my manhood. It's just never been that big a deal in my mind.

But until my association with Joe Murray and his buddies in Lufkin, there was always a faint anxiety I often felt in the company of men I admired. There was this persistent tinge of self-consciousness or insecurity—a gnawing suspicion that I didn't really know how to act or what to say. This makes me think of my relationship with Willie Nelson. Many people, both inside and outside Willie's circle, seemed to believe Willie and I were the closest of friends. Willie and I did talk a lot and we spent a considerable amount of time together during the Texas music uprising. Willie made a point of inviting me places—including to his home a time or two, and he asked me to do the programs for his July Fourth picnics. Stuff like that. But the truth was Willie and I were never that close. I think my awe of his talent got in the way.

My usual modus operandi for solving that sort of dilemma—feeling uneasy around men I admired the most—was to claim to have something else important to do and leaving after a relatively short time. And sometimes by reacting aggressively against some of their confident declarations. There also were many times when I simply kept my mouth shut and listened—even when profoundly perceptive commentary came to mind.

Don't misunderstand. I've always had as many men friends as the next fellow whose basic introverted nature clashed with his yen to teach everybody how to act right and think right. This yen is one more reason, no doubt, I was drawn to teaching and journalism—especially the editorial writing part. But, most of the time, all my life, I remained inside my protective bubble and never understood why. For that reason, and maybe others I haven't yet revealed even to myself, I was just a little bit surprised when I realized that Joe Murray, a man I met for the first time when I was over fifty, was probably the closest male friend I ever had. I have also come to realize, of course, that Joe's intrinsic unselfishness, good humored curiosity, dog-loving loyalty and unsurpassed ability to simply be good company had as much to do with my judging him "the best friend I ever had" as any soul-searching realizations or changes in my own outlook.

It may be that it was one of those "which came first the chicken or the egg" situations—or rather which caused what. Was it Joe's deep-seated honesty, his guileless generosity, etc.? Or was it the change in my own attitude? My maturity, you could say. I did a lot of thinking, a kind of meditating, in Lufkin—a lot of self-examination. I called it doing my yogi.

It's a little alarming to realize you've gone through over half your life without having done much serious self-examination—without actually facing and analyzing what makes you who you are—what works and doesn't work. I discovered, to my chagrin, that, no way around it—I had passed through fifty-odd years with little or no planning. Looking back, I saw that in fact, I had applied for a job only twice in my life. The other times when I made career changes, it was because somebody offered me something I thought would be more interesting than what I was doing at the time. It has been a good life, an interesting life. One that has taken me from Texas to Mississippi to New York, through Washington, D. C., and Harvard University, and I had counted more than one living legend among my running buddies. And now here I was in Lufkin, Texas. It occurred to me that no one ever became a living legend without staying in one place for a long time. Something I had never done.

Joe Murray had lived in Lufkin all his life. ("So far," he would say.) His father had worked at the *Daily News* as a linotype operator. Joe worked various jobs at the Lufkin newspaper as a high school student and during summer vacations when he was attending the University of North Texas in Denton. He worked awhile—a couple of years maybe—as East Texas correspondent for the *Houston Chronicle* and then went back to the *Lufkin Daily News* where he earned his way up to editor and publisher, before winning the Pulitzer Prize and

becoming a senior writer for Cox Newspapers of Atlanta, the
outfit that bought the Lufkin paper in 1977.

As a columnist for Cox, Joe could go just about anywhere
he wanted to go. He crossed the United States several times
in trains, planes and by automobile—visited Russia several
times—spent time in Cuba, Rio de Janeiro, Paris, London,
Ireland, Canada, South Africa—and just about every other
place he could think of he had ever wanted to visit. Or he
could stay at home and write about his East Texas neighbors.

Joe has this knack, this talent, for finding the town's, or
city's or village's most interesting characters and getting them
to talk freely about themselves, their lives, their countries,
political conflicts and anything and everything else that interests them. "How do you do that," I once asked. "It's what I
do," he answered. Among the things Joe and I found we had
in common was a love of good stories, telling them and hearing them. Joe said there are two kinds of people: joke tellers
and story tellers. We laughed at a good joke, but we preferred
a good story every time. Preferably a true story, or one that
stretched the truth just a little to make it a better story.

Sometimes Joe's best stories feature himself and never
appear in his columns.

For two or three weeks, a few years back, Joe had severe
headaches off and on. He was getting worried because he
could touch a certain place on his thigh and his head would
hurt fiercely. His doctor in Lufkin suggested a CAT scan to
check out Joe's brain waves, but he refused. He said he didn't
like the idea of getting stuck in one of those microwave dealies.
Anyhow, he admitted, he was afraid of what they might find.
Not long after that, while on one of his trips—this time through
the South, searching for the "quiet people" George Bush kept
talking about so much in his campaign for President. The

first night out, Joe was lying on this strange motel bed when the pain hit hard. By morning, he had sworn he would let the doctor do anything he wanted as soon as he got back home. After another night of piercing pain in his head, Joe had resorted to praying. He promised God he would send five thousand dollars to this mission in South Africa he knew about if God would get him past this without a life-threatening tumor or cancer of any kind. Joe knew about the mission through correspondence with a nun in a cloistered convent in Lufkin. When he got back to Lufkin, he went straight to his doctor and told him about his suffering and how when he touched his thigh the pain would shoot across his head something terrible. The doctor stuck his finger in Joe's mouth and wiggled a newly-arrived wisdom tooth, and the pain stopped and never returned.

But there remained hanging over Joe's head the covenant he'd made about the five thousand dollars. After a few days and nights of struggling with himself, he finally went ahead and sent the money. A promise is a promise to Joe Murray.

Joe's influence as a serious reporter, columnist and editor who pushed his reporters instead of holding them back, resulted in a number of Joe Murray alums going on to become stars on larger papers. Ken Herman went to the Associated Press bureau in Austin and then became bureau chief for the *Houston Chronicle* there. He could have gone to any number of other large dailies, but he didn't want to leave Austin. Heber Taylor, who did just about every job at the *Lufkin Daily News*, including accompanying Joe on several of his column-harvesting trips, is managing editor of the Galveston daily. Christie Harlan went to the *Dallas Morning News*, then the *Wall Street Journal*, and last I heard, was at Yale on a special fellowship. Phil Latham, Joe's Managing Editor, is now Editor of the Marshall, Texas, daily—a new Cox acquisition. And there are a number of other outstanding graduates of the Joe Murray regime in Lufkin. These are just the ones who passed through during my time there.

Life Is Just a
Bowl of Cherries

Townes Van Zandt, one of our foremost singing songwriters, died in January of 1997, almost twenty years after the death of novelist Billie Lee Brammer. Townes died at his home, apparently of a heart attack. Billie Lee OD'd in his apartment in Austin in 1978. Townes had been living up near Nashville before he died.

I only met him a couple of times, but felt like I knew him because other Texas picker poets told me so much about him, always with a lot of emotion—Lee Clayton, Jerry Jeff Walker, Guy Clark, and other first class songwriters, some better known by the public than others, but all known for singing mostly their own stuff. What they all told me about the man had a common theme: Townes Van Zandt was a major influence on their writing and on their decision to take songwriting seriously. No matter who else they cited as influencing them— most mentioned Willie and Jerry Jeff—they always included Townes Van Zandt.

Townes was fifty-two when his heart knocked him out. Brammer was about the same age when he OD'd. Both had pushed it to the limit most of their lives here, meantime producing musical poetry and prose that will live long after them, probably long after the rest of us have passed from our lives in their present aspect. Neither Townes nor Billie Lee was as famous with the general public as they were among fellow writers and performers. Perhaps Townes's most widely known song was "Pancho and Lefty" as interpreted by Willie Nelson and Merle Haggard. But he wrote hundreds of songs recorded by other musicians. One of my particular favorites is "If I Needed You."

John Henry Faulk, one of the older and wiser Maddogs who helped defeat the blacklisters back in the McCarthy era and wrote a good book about it (*Fear on Trial*) died in 1990 of cancer.

Both Gary Cartwright and Dan Jenkins have endured heart bypass surgery. A. C. Greene had a whole new heart transplanted in him. Larry McMurtry has lived through at least one bypass. And so it seems to be going these days. You don't know who will be added to the list next. But that's life, as the philosophical types say. Time is the enemy, if you think only in terms of enjoying the best parts of living now.

It's one of my theories that the spans of our lives here are measured because all the changes we inevitably experience as time goes by would drive us crazy if our lives were stretched across many more years. Who knows what television and computer mechanics will develop in the coming decades? I don't even want to think about it.

And what in the world are we going to do with all the people who will be trying to scratch out a living on this planet in, say, fifty years? There's damn near not enough room here now. Every time I see one of the smug reports telling us how many more people there are today in Texas than there were yesterday, I get a little claustrophobic. But there always seems to be another politician or one more Chamber of Commerce cheerleader declaring the benefits of unchecked growth. That kind of short term thinking has landed us in the present condition of having to rebuild our inner cities, suffer the consequences, pay the penalty, or all of the above, or else.

We're just not dying fast enough, as hard as that may be to face. As I face it in my deep mind, I find my thoughts going back to Big Daddy's then startling statement: "You probably can't tell by looking, but I've been scared all my life." And I tell myself that my old friends and I are moving into that zone where fear of death or disablement might start influencing the way we live our lives, if we're not careful, and I wonder how my old running buddies are taking it, especially with every report that another old amigo has died or come damn close to death.

I don't see the old Maddog bunch much anymore, but nevertheless, I can tell you with confidence that none of them is drastically inhibited by fears of death. But apparently, death is a mystery few writers can resist exploring at some time or another. McMurtry has always written stories with death as a major character or dominant symbol. Of all the Texas writers of that generation—all card-carrying Maddogs, in other words—McMurtry is probably the one most intrigued by death. Perhaps as others from that brotherhood of writers and performers grow older, they will find themselves examining its mysteries—each in his own individual style, of course.

After Gary Cartwright survived a heart attack and I don't know how many bypasses back in 1988, he got himself back in shape and wound up writing a book about it called *Heartwise Guy*. Everybody who has lived hard ought to read it and heed it.

Clogged arteries and all notwithstanding, most Texas Maddog writers are still too young to be worrying a whole lot about death and disabling disease, except, perhaps, in connection with their diets and lack of exercise. These days being in your fifties or sixties doesn't necessarily mean you're too old to cut the mustard, as we used to say in Lubbock. But it probably means the mustard gives you heartburn, so you usually substitute fat-free mayonnaise. But that's better than the alternative.

It may also mean that you have kids as old as you were when you received your Maddog, Inc. membership card, and are now fervently hoping he, or she, has more sense than you did at that age, but the odds against that seem to keep climbing every day.

The Maddogs, once regarded as the young rebels of Texas literature and music, are now looked upon as the Old Bulls. One of the big changes is that back when the Old Bulls were young, there weren't any women writers in that rabble. Now there are several notable women writers around the state. In point of fact, in recent years the Texas women writers have been producing some of the best writing to come out of the state.

As for me, as I settle into my dotage with the woman I love, who loves me beyond all reason, I find myself thinking: "I'm not scared any more."

But looking back over my life, I realize that damned if I hadn't been scared most of the time, although I didn't really realize it. Maybe being scared and not realizing it is the same as not be scared at all, but I don't think so. At least I wasn't too scared to finish this book, as I obviously had been on other books previously.

A few years back, Cartwright and I wound up at the same party and, since we hadn't seen each other in awhile, got off by ourselves to talk. Gary said he'd heard I was writing a novel, and I admitted I was. "What's it about?" he asked innocently— or maybe not so innocently. I stammered something, added something else, then something else, and finally closed with the ever popular: "Well, it's kinda hard to put it in just a few words."

In the years I had known Gary—Jap—he had become semi-famous as a man who was able to get to the meat of things quicker than most people. I soon realized Jap hadn't changed. "According to what I've heard," Jap said matter-of-factly, "if you can't tell what it's about in one sentence, you don't have it under control."

I frowned and passed this tidbit of wisdom off as a joke, and Cartwright, perhaps a kinder and gentler Cartwright, went along with it, and we dropped the subject. Later, the more I thought about it, the more I became convinced that not being able to tell what it was about in one sentence, or at least two or three short sentences, might just be the reason the New York editor kept telling me to rewrite it.

Thus, when I decided to do this book, the first thing I did was figure out what it was about. (I've also taken to reading the instructions on packages before attempting to use their contents.) So: This book is about a group of Texas writers who became friends early in their careers (some had been friends as far back as high school) and remained friends through the years that saw them producing a lot of good journalism and some reasonably serious fiction and music. More handsomely for some and less so for others, but—individually, and as a group—were far enough ahead of their time to break down some intellectual and emotional stumbling blocks for those coming along behind to enable them, perhaps, to write better and with more confidence because those psychological barriers were already battered down. There it is—a long sentence, granted—but a single sentence nevertheless.

It should be superfluous to say that everything you have read in this book is the way I saw it, as seen and heard through my eyes and ears. My stories, no doubt, will conflict with those told by others who were right there and may have participated. I've heard and read many of those other versions myself. That doesn't bother me—I know what I saw and heard, and did.

I must add that many Maddogs who write have been accused lately of carrying on a Good Ole Boy alliance that may have kept them from being honestly critical of each other's work. They allegedly have been prone to pat each other's backs with jacket blurb endorsements without even reading the books. This kind of clannishness is said, by some, to have been going on among the Old Bulls of Texas writing for some time.

I hope this book will prove those accusations to be entirely true. I trust, also, that this book will explain, or reveal, why such accusations are well-founded and why, in fact, a Good Ole Boy network was inevitable. People tend to forget how difficult it was just a few decades ago to get anything started in the hinterlands in creative writing and music. And, until relatively recently, Texas was a hinterland province, no doubt about it.

I have declared a time or two that for years after returning to Texas in the early 1960s from the rapidly sinking *New York Herald Tribune*, I was acting a role that didn't fit me comfortably. Not long before he died, Hondo Crouch, the famed imagineer of Luckenbach, Texas, and the world, expressed it more clearly than anybody I've heard since.

"We all, you and me and everybody else," Hondo said one night at his country home after a Jerry Jeff Walker taping in nearby Luckenbach, "go into our acts the minute we walk out the door every morning."

Hondo went on to theorize that we're all acting in movies of our own scripting and what we're really doing is (I've added some of my own interpretation of Hondo's wisdom here), waiting around to grab one of the best roles. Sometimes we get overly anxious and grab roles that don't suit us, or let others—a group of our friends, maybe—miscast us as characters that don't really suit us.

Those lucky souls who manage to play the characters they want to be and are suited for, are the ones we say "have it all together," and such as that. This may or may not be the whole truth, but if it seems to be true, to them and others, then maybe it's close enough to be the truth, maybe even the whole truth. But those of us who have tried unsuccessfully to fit into roles assigned to us by some casting director—who only thinks he or she knows us—are the ones who, at times anyway, obviously didn't have it "all together" yet. Could be.

● ● ●

It was late, that night at Hondo's, that much I do remember very well. Or I suppose it'd be more accurate to say it was early, since it must have been getting close to sunrise. Susan Walker and Susanna Clark (she and her partner, Guy Clark, had flown down that day for Jerry Jeff's taping at Luckenbach) had huddled after looking into the weary but determined-to-hang-in-there look in Hondo's eyes, and assured him that he shouldn't feel it was necessary to stay on his feet until the last man or woman fell on his or her face. (They might have more precisely said: until only Jerry Jeff and Shrake were still standing.)

So, Hondo finally did sneak off and get a little sleep before he had to arise and put on his Sunday-go-to-meeting cowboy getup and supervise an auction in San Antonio that afternoon to raise funds for an orphanage he just happened to know was on the brink of financial disaster. (Hondo reported later that day, with a rueful twinkle in his eyes, that he saw both the tragic and ironical sides to the fact that the auction got rained out.) Anyhow, before going off to bed just before dawn, Hondo asked me if I'd ever heard his theme song.

I said I hadn't, so he sang it just for me, complete with the appropriate gestures. It was "Life is Just a Bowl of Cherries," sung to a very slow tempo, his hands framing his broad, clownish forced smile, with his hands, palms out, like Shirley Temple used to do.

Index